THE MANDAEANS—

Baptizers of Iraq and Iran

THE MANDAEANS—

Baptizers of Iraq and Iran

Karen Baker

Foreword by Amal Bejjani

WIPF & STOCK · Eugene, Oregon

THE MANDAEANS—BAPTIZERS OF IRAQ AND IRAN

Copyright © 2017 Karen Baker. All rights reserved. Except for brief quotations in critical publications or reviews, no part of this book may be reproduced in any manner without prior written permission from the publisher. Write: Permissions, Wipf and Stock Publishers, 199 W. 8th Ave., Suite 3, Eugene, OR 97401.

Wipf & Stock
An Imprint of Wipf and Stock Publishers
199 W. 8th Ave., Suite 3
Eugene, OR 97401

www.wipfandstock.com

PAPERBACK ISBN: 978-1-5326-1970-0
HARDCOVER ISBN: 978-1-4982-4621-7
EBOOK ISBN: 978-1-4982-4620-0

Manufactured in the U.S.A.   SEPTEMBER 26, 2017

Originally published as *The Hidden Peoples of the World: The Mandaeans of Iraq, An exploration of the Mandaeans of Iraq: their history, beliefs, community organization and the effect of the 21st Century Diaspora,* VDM Verlag Dr. Müller, Saarbrücken, Germany, 2009

No part of this book may be reproduced, stored in a retrieval system, or transmitted in any form of by any means—electronic, mechanical, photocopy, recording or otherwise—without prior written permission of the publisher, except brief quotations used in connection with reviews in magazines or newspapers.

Scripture quotations are taken from the Holy Bible, New International Version, All rights reserved.

Photos: Provided courtesy of Jody Miller.

Cover photo courtesy of Jody Miller. The *drabsa* is a banner used during the baptismal ritual.

To my beloved husband Verne,

who has modeled life-long learning and
who has been my best friend, supporter, encourager, and advocate,
and especially for our partnership with the hidden peoples of the world.

In memory of my mother, Elaine Newcomb,

who gave me a love for learning by modeling life-long learning.

Other books in the Hidden Peoples of the World series by Karen Baker:

The Balkars of Southern Russia and Their Deportation (1944–57)

The Balkars of Southern Russia and Their Deportation (1944–57rr.), (Russian-language version)

Author proceeds from this book will be donated to Global Partners in Peace and Development to serve the Mandaean people of Iraq and Iran.

Contents

List of Tables | viii

Map of Historic Locations of Mandaeans | ix

Foreword by Amal Bejjani | xi

Preface | xv

Acknowledgments | xvii

    1   Introduction | 1

    2   History and Sources: Gnosticism | 15

    3   History and Sources: Mandaeism | 26

    4   Membership and Community | 64

    5   Authority and Organization | 71

    6   Rituals and Holidays | 79

    7   Signs and Symbols | 90

    8   Conclusion: Opportunities | 95

Bibliography | 105

Index | 109

List of Tables

Table 1. Mandaeism vis-à-vis Gnosticism | 33

Table 2. Mandaeism vis-à-vis Judaism | 38

Table 3. Mandaeism vis-à-vis Roman Catholicism | 43

Table 4. Mandaeism vis-à-vis Islam | 50

Table 5. Mandaeism vis-à-vis Three Major World Religions | 57

Table 6. Mandaean Priests vis-à-vis Jewish Priests | 76

Map of Historic Locations of Mandaeans

MOST OF THE IRAQI Mandaeans live(d) in southern Iraq, near the marshes of the Tigris and Euphrates Rivers; a smaller community of Mandaeans lived and worked in Baghdad prior to 2003, where there was a ready market for their jewelry. The Iranian communities of Mandaeans live in southwestern Iran, near the marshes of the Karun River.

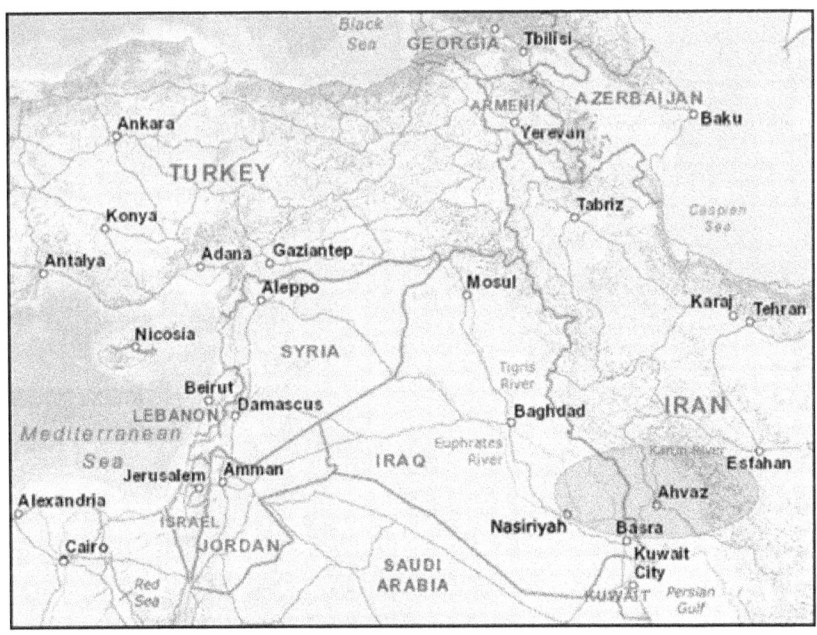

NATIONAL GEOGRAPHIC CREATIVE, used with permission

Foreword

DURING THE YEARS OF our church-planting ministry among refugees in the Middle East in the aftermath of the First Gulf War, we encountered an ethno-religious people group called the Mandaeans (also known as Sabaeans), who claim to be followers of John the Baptist. That was the first time we encountered this group, which surely numbers among the "families of the earth" to be blessed by the Messiah of the Abrahamic promise (Gen 12:3), and among the *panta ta ethne* of Matthew 28:19.

Since we had not heard of the Mandaeans before, we knew next to nothing about them. This is how, in God's sovereignty, the encounter happened. We had started a school for refugee children, and one day a lady came to our door asking if we'd accept "non-Christian" (her expression) children. We said we certainly did, and would. The next morning she brought her children to our school, and said she would also volunteer to teach math with us (as she had been a math teacher in her country), if we'd accept her. We said we would.

At our school we started every morning with Chapel, which consisted of a few children's songs, a Bible story, and prayer. This mother and her children (later followed by her husband) were the first converts from the Mandaeans in that ministry. But little did we know that God's Spirit was on the move in a special way among Mandaean refugees in our area. For shortly after this family's conversion, several of their relatives who came to our city with their families also came to Christ.

Over time we came into contact with many more Mandaeans. At one point, at least half the children in the school were Mandaeans. Interestingly, a cotton candy street-seller advertised our school in a neighborhood of our

FOREWORD

city highly populated by Mandaean refugee families, and the numbers of Mandaean children attending the school swelled virtually overnight!

Eventually, when the church was well established with leadership and a healthy vision, several Mandaean families were baptized and were among those who served and reached out to the various groups we worked amongst. This did not happen without a measure of opposition from their community and religious leaders. There was an instance where one Mandaean priest made a false profession of faith in Christ and volunteered to teach language at our school (where we taught Arabic, English, math, science, and Bible), only to spy on his fellow Mandaeans who were showing interest in Christ. He began to visit them privately, and to discourage them from sending their children to the school and attending church. But we found out about his deception and stratagem, confronted him, and asked him not to teach at the school anymore. He continued to attempt to sabotage our work, but God worked it out that he and his family traveled to Australia shortly thereafter.

Later, as many of these Mandaean background believers became refugees in various Western countries, ranging from Europe to North America to Australia, they continued to follow Christ and witness to his gospel.

We were eventually ousted from the country where we had labored for many years, and the Lord led us to a city in Midwestern America, where we now continue our church-planting work among refugees on this side of the Refugee Highway. There are many Mandaean families in our city, and they too are being reached with the good news, and a few believers are found among them.

Mandaeans are now found in many of our cities in North America, with the largest concentrations being found in Worcester, Massachusetts; San Antonio, Texas; and Toronto, Canada. Many are continuing to leave their homelands due to hardship and persecution. It seems many times the Lord disperses people groups and brings them through many troubles to a saving knowledge of himself.

To my knowledge, Karen Baker's book on the Mandaeans of the Ahvaz region of southeastern Iraq and southwestern Iran is the first of its kind: it is the only contemporary, well-researched work on this ethno-religious people group in the English language. The Mandaeans are a minority that has undergone persecution on and off throughout their history, though their persecution has been heavier in recent decades, both in Saddam's Iraq and post-Saddam Iraq, as well as in Khomeini's Iran and post-Khomeini

FOREWORD

Iran. As a result, their dispersion is now far and wide, and though for many centuries they have ranked among the least-reached groups of the world, their dispersion has led to the beginnings of their evangelization. Part of our story, as related above, ties in with Karen Baker's research, as during our work among Iraqi refugees we came across Mandaeans for the first time, and some became followers of the Lord Jesus Christ; hitherto they had come short of following Christ, as they counted themselves followers of John the Baptist, whom they consider superior to Christ by virtue of having baptized him.

This book is a unique work that will aid in understanding the Mandaeans and by God's grace lead to more spreading of the gospel among them for God's glory. May we see more Mandaeans reached for Christ in North America, Europe, and Australia, and may they eventually run the good news right back to those parts of Iraq and Iran where their origins lie.

Rev. Amal Bejjani, missionary to Arabic-speaking refugees since 1988

Preface

My interest in the Mandaeans dates back to the early 2000s when I met "followers of John the Baptist" who were refugees in Amman, Jordan. This attribution intrigued me to the point where I wanted to know more about these people and their beliefs.

I was able to research this people group during my years as a graduate student at Liberty University in Lynchburg, Virginia. This book is the result of what began as several research papers and developed into my Master's thesis; this version revisits the original thesis and updates it with new information. The initial premise argued that the status of Iraqi Mandaeans, who were fleeing their native country and becoming refugees by the thousands, presented an unprecedented opportunity for the gospel message. The Great Commission requires taking the gospel message to every people group in the world. However, the Mandaeans have been an inaccessible, hidden, unknown, misunderstood sect until the present time.

This book evaluates the history and the current situation of Mandaeans through academic journals and books, consultation with missionaries and workers among Mandaeans, and interviews with Mandaeans and Mandaean refugees. As a result of their physical isolation deep within the Muslim world of Iraq and Iran, and their philosophical and cultural isolation based on their emphasis on secret truths, the Mandaean sect has not previously been exposed to the gospel. Their unique status as refugees has created the first opportunity in centuries for Mandaeans to have the opportunity to hear the gospel.

The evaluation of the Mandaeans' potential receptivity toward the gospel is based on five comparative categories by which religious motivations

Preface

and ethics can be understood. These categories are: history and origins of the religion; membership and community of the group; authority and organization; rituals and holidays; and signs and symbols. The history and origin of Mandaeism are divided into two parts. The first investigates Mandaeism's relationship to the Gnosticism of the first through third centuries AD. The second evaluates the syncretic adaptations of Mandaeism to Judaism, Christianity, and Islam. Ultimately, the thesis has proven that though changes are painstakingly slow, Mandaean refugees who have encountered the gospel of the New Testament have responded in ways which are similar to those of other individuals. Sometimes the information falls on fertile ground; other times, it is not nourished into conversion. Yet the mandate to take the gospel message to every people, tribe, nation, and tongue continues to motivate Christians to share what they have learned with those who have not heard the good news. Thus the Mandaeans, an historically inaccessible people group, continue to be in an unparalleled, unique situation to receive the truth of the gospel message due to the continuing Diaspora.

A recent visit with a refugee family who has lived in America for over twenty years revealed that my husband and I are their "only American friends." How tragic that these people can live in our neighborhoods, attend our schools, work in our communities, and yet have no meaningful relationships with native-born American Christians. My heart's prayer is that through reading this book, the reader will become aware of "neighbors" who need to not only have friends, but to hear the Christian message in love.

Acknowledgments

No book, especially one that involves research, can be wholly attributed to the author. In this particular case, I had professors at Liberty University Seminary and School of Religion who coaxed details I would have never dreamed to ask. I especially thank those who were involved in the crafting of the master's thesis which led to this publication, particularly Dr. Carl Deimer and Dr. Michael Jones. I would be remiss if I didn't mention the Liberty University Research Library's Graduate Research Assistant, Randy Miller, who has been extraordinarily helpful, assuming a prominent role in details and methods unknown to me. I still consider him a dear friend and colleague in my endeavor to learn more about the hidden peoples of the world. I also thank the missionaries and the Mandaeans who cannot be named for security reasons, but all of whom added immeasurably to the understanding and depth of this book by sharing their insights, stories, experiences, and emotions.

My deepest gratitude goes to the author of everything, my Lord and Savior Jesus Christ, who put the idea into motion and provided the means to travel, health to pursue the stories, resources for the research, and affirmations at many milestones along the way.

1

Introduction

INTRODUCTION

THE UNREST IN THE Middle East has brought unprecedented opportunities to reach the unreached for Christ. The Mandaeans, a small gnostic sect, have been located primarily in southern Iraq and in southwestern Iran for centuries. This people group is classified as one of over 6,500 unreached people groups. Being defined as unreached by mission organizations means that less than two percent of the population is identified as evangelical Christians. It is a "people group among which there is no indigenous community of believing Christians with adequate numbers and resources to evangelize the group without outside assistance."[1] Two percent of the indigenous population has been used by the Joshua Project as the minimum percentage of a population necessary in order to impact the entire group.

The unreached status of the Mandaeans comes first from their geographic isolation in Iraq and Iran, historically making them physically inaccessible to missionary efforts. Second, their hostility to outsiders has prevented influence even from Arab Christians within Iraq and Persian Christians in Iran. Third, their gnostic belief system has been relatively unknown to Christian organizations even to the present time. Thus, usual

---

1. Joshua Project, https://joshuaproject.net/help/definitions#unreached. The Joshua Project provides information on people groups that have the least exposure to the gospel and the least Christian presence in their midst. The organization compiles and updates the work of mission researchers in order to bring definition to the unfinished task of the Great Commission to accelerate the gospel's impact into each of the least-reached people groups. This information is provided to mission agencies to assist as they develop their strategies to reach the lost.

methods of evangelism have not penetrated this sect. Their belief system is not an aberration of Judeo-Christian doctrines, nor is it a derivation of any of the major world religions such as Hinduism, Buddhism, Islam, or even tribal or animistic practices. Because the Mandaean beliefs are in a category of their own and because of their traditional isolation from and hostility toward outsiders, reaching them has been virtually impossible geographically and philosophically.

The quest to discover who the Mandaeans are is not easily satisfied because, first, ascertaining the name of the sect is a challenge. For every name, there are different spellings; for every spelling, there are different groups, some of which have no relationship to the people of this study. The names used include: Sabia Al-Mandaean, usually shortened to Sabian; Sabaean; Subba (meaning baptizers, those who immerse themselves in water); Sabba; Mendaia or Mendai; Sabbi; and St. John Christians, later corrected to John the Baptist rather than the Apostle John.[2]

Part of the reason for this confusion is the secretive nature of the people themselves. Although some have revealed some of their secrets to various authors, the information is not always consistent. Even within the sect, knowledge of beliefs, practices, and history among its adherents is neither widely understood nor consistent. Their self-identification varies based on the listener. To someone they consider unfriendly, they will call themselves one of the various forms of Sabaean, but within their community and to friendly outsiders, they identify themselves as Mandaeans.[3] This book refers to this people group as Mandaean unless a direct quote uses another name.

Second, further complicating the matter is the fact that "Mandaean" refers to one who both belongs to a specific ethnic group and adheres to a

---

2. Miller, Email to author, 25 Jan 2006; "Islamic historians referred to all pagans as 'Sabaeans.'" Lupieri, *Last Gnostics*, 85. "The Mandaeans have always played up the similarity in sound between *subba* and *sabiah* (as referenced in the Qur'an) in order to obtain a much-desired recognition from the local (Muslim) lords" (67). Sabbi is the name used by the Arabs and Persians for this people (95). These names are all the more confused by the willingness of the Mandaeans to rewrite their history based on the favor/oppression that might be facing them. In fact, it was the Portuguese who aligned the Mandaeans with John the Baptist, "since in their rituals, together with their name and the appearance of Christianity, there have mixed together many superstitious ceremonies that have a Jewish air about them" (87).

3. Wisam, interviewed by author 16 Oct 2006. This was also the author's experience when meeting a jeweler in Dubai. When asked if he was Mandaean, he said, "no;" when asked if he was Sabaean, he asked how I knew these names!

INTRODUCTION

specific religious belief. "Once they have abandoned their specific religious identity, they cease to exist as a separate ethnic group."[4] Thus, finding Mandaeans who may have converted to another religion is difficult as they may no longer respond to the ethnicity of Mandaeism in a census. The Mandaeans have lived in seclusion for centuries along the marshes of the Tigris and Euphrates Rivers in Iraq and the Karun River in Iran. The world around them, primarily Muslim, has had little influence on their ancient practices. However, since the early years of the twenty-first century, the tumult of the Middle East has forced their dispersion to twenty-five countries around the world.

The total, worldwide population of Mandaeans is difficult to estimate for three reasons: 1) conflicting and unavailable information, and the lack of specifics on this population within the greater populations of the countries they live in (especially Iraq and Iran); 2) identification of Mandaeans who are no longer in Iraq, Iran, or the Middle East; 3) lack of clarity regarding the identity of Mandaeans who have left the sect. Using the most conservative and most current estimates in 2017, there are between 30,000–70,000 Mandaeans worldwide.[5]

Population distribution is even harder to obtain due to political unrest in Iraq and Iran, and emigration patterns that are difficult to track.[6] The countries with the highest estimated numbers of Mandaeans are: Sweden (10,500), Australia (10,000), Iran (10,000), Canada (6,000), Iraq (5,000), the United States (4,000), and Holland (4,000). Within the United States, there are small Mandaean communities in Michigan, California, Florida, Texas, Nebraska, Massachusetts, and Maryland.[7] However, even these locations fluctuate in the United States due to internal migration and the lack of official tracking of immigrants who are in America legally. Finally, the term Mandaean refers both to one who belongs to a specific ethnic group and to one who adheres to a specific religious belief. Their ethnicity is tied to their religion, and if one leaves the religious sect, he is no longer considered ethnically Mandaean.[8]

---

4. Lupieri, *Last Gnostics*, 5.

5. The Mandaean Human Rights Group estimated 30,000–43,000 Iraqi Mandaeans. "Mandaeans of Iraq since 2015," Mandaean Human Rights Group, 28 Mar 2017. Wikipedia estimated 60,000–70,000 Mandaeans including Iranian. "Mandaeans," https://en.widipedia.org/wiki/Mandaeans.

6. Buckley, *The Mandaeans*, 6.

7. Bejjani, discussion with author, 07 Mar 2005 and 27 Feb 2006.

8. Lupieri, *The Mandaeans*, 5.

The Mandaeans—Baptizers of Iraq and Iran

Pre-2003 estimates of the worldwide population of Mandaeans ranged from 60,000 to 100,000. Because of the inability to convert into the sect, and the decreasing access to priests throughout all of these locations, continuing their rituals and traditions has become increasingly untenable. "After more than 2,000 years of practicing their gnostic faith almost entirely in Iraq and Iran, some Mandaean-Americans fear their ancient beliefs may fade in the U.S. unless they can agree on a cultural course that keeps traditions intact while dealing with the pressures of American society."[9] Some predict that the Mandaeans are on the brink of extinction; that the Mandaeans will be fully decimated within 30 years; or certainly by the end of this century.[10]

The three wars in Iraq and the ongoing conflict have had the potential of bringing not only physical freedom, but also spiritual freedom to the Iraqi Mandaeans. The Persian Gulf War (1990–91), Operation Desert Storm (1990–91), Operation Freedom (2003–11), and the presence of ISIS (2014–present) have produced the largest Diaspora of Mandaeans in history, scattering Mandaeans throughout the world.

---

9. Associated Press, "Ancient Iraqi Mandaean sect struggles to keep culture in Michigan," mlive, 01 Jul 2009, http://www.mlive.com/news/detroit/index.ssf/2009/07/ancient_iraqi_mandaean_sect_st.html.

10. Sly, "Ancient Iraqi Sect is a Silent Casualty of War"; "Syria"; Hanish, "Christians, Yazidis, and Mandaeans in Iraq," 12.

INTRODUCTION

Persecution of this people group began with Saddam Hussein's forces. In the aftermath of the Iraqi government's demise, sectarian and criminal groups, extremists from both Shiite and Sunni Muslims, have persistently targeted the Mandaeans. Some of the methods used to harass and intimidate both adults and children have included: rape of women in front of their husbands; forced marriage of Mandaean women and young girls to Muslim men; rape of young girls; forced male circumcision (a sin in their religion); kidnapping for ransom; illegal confiscation of property; bombing and burning of their homes and shops; executions for refusal to convert to Islam; forced circumcision of young boys, making them ineligible to be Mandaeans; pressure to evacuate their homes in a specific time, such as twenty-four hours; and rape and murder of women for the lack of a hijab. Harassment and intimidation occur at all levels of Mandaean society, from the professional and business class (teachers, lawyers, doctors, goldsmiths), to children in schools. A common method of harassment is the finger-pointing of other students, calling them unclean and dirty because they don't act like Muslims. They have also suffered discrimination by the courts, been treated as second-class citizens, and experienced discrimination in jobs and employment. Furthermore, crimes against Mandaeans, as a minority in Iraqi society, are less likely to be effectively investigated or punished. "The foremost reasons for minorities leaving Iraq are safety and security, direct threat or immediate danger, religious freedom, and hard economic conditions associated with war and destruction in Iraq after the 2003 invasion.[11] Clashes between other groups in Iraq, such as the Kurds and the Arabs of northern Iraq, and ISIS, which has wreaked havoc on the whole of Iraq, have left the Mandaeans homeless and hopeless. "As far as the Mandaeans are concerned, the insecurity and unfamiliarity of a life in exile and permanent separation from their homeland is preferable to going back to Iraq. . . . It is impossible for the time being for them to go home. The risk is too great."[12]

Further complicating the situation for the Mandaeans is their culture, a tight-knit, secretive community. Refugees are targeted individually for harassment, and are not given immigration opportunities based on group or communal needs, but rather on individual families. Thus, relocating around the world has resulted in small communities, without the support

---

11. Ibid., 13.
12. Reinke, "Mandaeans in Iraq," 8.

and leadership that is necessary to maintain their religion and their culture. For example, in Worcester, Massachusetts, there are 150 refugees who

> have formed the largest Iraqi Mandaean refugee settlement in the United States. . . . [W]ithout a permanent priest or proper place of worship for the next generation, the refugees worry their tiny, ancient religion is facing extinction. "We're saving the people but killing the faith," said Wisam Breegi, a Mandaean doctor and U.S. citizen who has helped bring dozens of Mandaean refugees to Massachusetts. "But right now we're in survival mode."[13]

In addition, Liz Sly agrees when she says, "Once Mandaeans reach the West, they are at risk of losing touch with their cultures and traditions. No overseas community numbers more than 4,000, and that is hardly enough to support their survival, scholars say."[14]

For most that flee Iraq, the first stop is Amman, Jordan, a country that has traditionally welcomed refugees awaiting relocation to other parts of the world. The Jordanian government does not allow Christian efforts toward its own Muslim population; however, Jordan welcomes humanitarian efforts to assist refugees with basic needs, including education and health care. This creates an opportunity to bring Christ's love to the Mandaeans in an environment that encourages them to be open to the gospel. In fact, after the Persian Gulf War, missionaries reported that more Iraqi refugees in Amman came to faith in Jesus Christ than the total evangelical Christian population of Jordan.[15]

Refugees are a growing population around the globe and represent opportunities for the gospel that might not otherwise be available. In fact, the crises that often create refugees are becoming more visible and compelling throughout the world, representing opportunities for which Christians must be prepared. Examples include wars, terrorism and lawlessness, earthquakes, volcanoes, tsunamis, hurricanes, and other natural disasters.

War can sometimes bring hope to the oppressed. Such has been the case for the Mandaeans who have lived in a closed society for centuries. Since the late twentieth century, Mandaeans have joined the thousands of Iraqis who have left their homeland in search of safety and opportunity in other countries. Additionally, Mandaeans from Iran have fled to the European Union, and from there to points beyond. The path of the Iranian

13. "Ancient religious group flees from Iraq; finds refuge in Mass."
14. Sly, "Ancient Iraqi Sect is a Silent Casualty of War."
15. Eenigenburg, Correspondence to author, 24 Jul 2006.

INTRODUCTION

Mandaeans is slightly different than the Iraqis, and because the majority of Mandaean refugees come from Iraq, the focus of this book will document their journey from the Middle East.

Published reports indicate that before these conflicts in Iraq, there were between 250,000 and 300,000 Iraqis in Jordan, although officials acknowledge that this is a conservative estimate. "The number of Iraqis could be much higher since Iraqis in Jordan doubt the benefits of registering with the UNHCR (United Nations High Commissioner for Refugees) and therefore fail to do so."[16] Bejjani estimated that "at the height of the Iraqi refugee situation in Jordan's capital, there were nearly a half million refugees in Amman."[17] The population of Amman at that time was 1.2 million, not including the refugees.[18] In the aftermath of "the two Gulf Wars, around one million Iraqis fled to Jordan. Years later, nearly half of these are unable or unwilling to return home."[19] Unfortunately, this number does not distinguish the Mandaeans from the total Iraqi refugee estimate. Most refugees desire to return to their homeland, as did most of the Shiite Muslims who had left under Saddam Hussein's regime. Of the Iraqis in Jordan before Operation Freedom, only 5,000 refugees were awaiting resettlement to another safe country. When Saddam Hussein's government was toppled in 2003, the Shiites returned to Iraq from Jordan in vast numbers, but refuges of other sects and ethnicities quickly replaced them. Jordan's agreement since 1998 has been to grant temporary asylum to refugees "for a maximum period of six months, after which they become illegal aliens, subject to daily fines and at risk of forced deportation back to Iraq. The *de facto* presence of refugees waiting for resettlement is tolerated by the authorities pending their departure, although they have no permission to work and they are subject to regular roundups."[20]

Most Iraqi refugees arrive in Amman with intact families and often with extended family members. Though on occasion men will leave ahead of their families to scope out opportunities, pave the way for emigration to other countries, or secure living quarters, most have fled Iraq as a family unit, taking only as many of their possessions as they can carry.

---

16. "Flight from Iraq," Human Rights Watch, 14.
17. Bejjani, discussion with author, 7 Mar 2005 and 27 Feb 2006.
18. Johnstone, *Operation World*, 326.
19. Mandryk, *Operation World*, 497.
20. "Flight from Iraq," 14.

In the refugee community, the playing field is leveled and the usual tensions and conflicts among various sectors of Iraqi society seem to be non-existent. In fact, these differences may be emphasized more in the press than actually exist in real life. "People groups have been played against one another, especially throughout the Ottoman rule through World War I, in order to maintain authority and control over these occupied lands. The British continued this method of control until they left after World War II."[21]

The social structures of refugee communities are often completely broken down. Safety and trust are lacking. There is distrust among members of the community, who fear traitors or informers; toward foreigners, especially Westerners; and toward the host country. Language barriers often create suspicions and prevent relationship-building.

Fear is pervasive among refugees because of: past experiences in their native country; military reprisals; intimidation; being forced to return to imprisonment or death in their home country; or an uncertain future.[22] Additionally, there is an "alarming tendency for exile to become long-term, if not permanent. This is something that dehumanizes, uproots people from their cultural milieu, leaves them in constant insecurity and leads to intractable social and security problems."[23]

The needs of all refugees, regardless of country of origin, religion, sect, occupation, education, or social status, are reduced to basic existence. The refugees in Amman live in very poor, substandard conditions. They cannot work legally. Health care is unavailable. Food is meager. Water is scarce. Education is not an option. Fear is rampant. Hope is illusive for refugees as their self-identity, dignity, safety, and security have all been ravaged.

The strategies used by missionaries for refugees as a group take precedence over strategies for a specific religious or people group since they are all in the same community and, facing many of the same issues, can potentially be reached with similar strategies. Outreach efforts that are culturally relevant, combined with a high degree of creative flexibility, are most effective in any given area. Takona has written on the importance of building relationships in sharing the gospel, stating that, "Any strategy should focus on reaching a people within the context of their needs rather than on the basis of preconceived methodologies."[24] She further emphasizes this notion

---

21. Bejjani, discussion with author, 7 Mar 2005 and 27 Feb 2006.
22. Flamm, "Refugee Ministry," 101.
23. Blume, "Refugees and Mission," 169.
24. Takona, "Strategies for Muslim Evangelization," 55–56.

INTRODUCTION

by quoting Dayton and Frazer's work in *Strategies for World Evangelism*, who write that "Evangelization always takes place in the context of needs."[25]

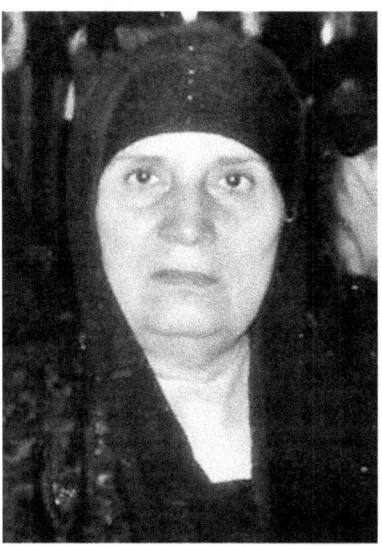

PURPOSE

The purpose of this book is to provide descriptive information to assist missionaries, mission agencies, and individuals or groups to better understand this specific unreached people group, the Mandaeans. The current dispersion of Mandaeans offers a window of opportunity to reach individual Mandaeans who are either refugees or have resettled throughout the world. Sources include representative academic materials, consultation with missionaries directly involved with the Mandaeans, and discussions with Mandaeans, some of whom have converted to Christianity. Since gnostic beliefs, and specifically Mandaean beliefs, are significantly different from what a Western evangelical Christian would normally encounter among Western nonbelievers, this book provides a description of their beliefs and practices and discusses how these factors could be used to initiate a conversation about biblical truths.

The Mandaeans, a sect that dates back to at least the first and second centuries after Christ, have lived in the southern portions of what is now

---

25. Ibid., 55–56.

The Mandaeans—Baptizers of Iraq and Iran

Iraq and Iran. Iraq was formed out of three former provinces of the Ottoman Empire in 1920. "From its earliest history, Iraq has been a passageway between East and West. Its borders are for the most part artificial, reflecting the interests of the Great Powers during the First World War."[26] Prior to the borders of these countries being formed at the end of World War I, the Mandaeans were one community. Lacking their own clearly defined territory, the Mandaeans have been distributed in communities between the two countries, along the banks of the Tigris and Euphrates Rivers in Iraq, and the Karun River in Iran.

They are mentioned in the Qur'an as Sabeans.[27] The Qur'an provides for *ahl al-kitab*, which is tolerance toward "people of the Book," "people who profess a religion recognized by Islam to have been of divine origin."[28] To be *ahl al-kitab* requires monotheism and a holy or divine book. The Mandaeans produced a written copy of their prayers and rituals in the *Ginza* and thus qualified as *ahl al-kitab* in the mid-seventh century.[29]

As the only surviving, practicing gnostic group in the world, the Mandaeans have been the subject of investigation regarding their origins and the influence of Judaism, Islam, and Christianity on their beliefs. Since they are a closed sect, allowing no converts and having little to do with the outside world, information about this group has been unavailable until the nineteenth century when several of their writings were translated from their original, ancient language. Similarly, physical access to the sect has been extremely difficult in their native locales in Iraq or Iran. Buckley noted, after her 1996 visit with Iranian Mandaeans, that "No scholar from the outside had come to visit the Mandaeans . . . since the 1930s. Most were amazed that someone in the outside world would know their religion."[30]

---

26. Marr, *The Modern History of Iraq*, 9.

27. Although a people named Sabeans are mentioned in several passages of the Old Testament, they are not related to the people group under discussion. The biblical Sabeans, antagonists of God's people, were from the area of present-day Yemen.

28. Muhibbu-Din, "Ahl Al-Kitab and Religious Minorities in the Islamic State," 111.

29. Buckley, *The Mandaeans*, 5; Drower, *The Mandeans*, 24. Lady Drower lived among the Mandaeans during the 1930s and 1940s when her husband was a British diplomat to the area. She recorded her findings and translated many of the Mandaean texts, becoming the preeminent source for twentieth-century scholars. The *Ginza* is the Mandaean holy book, divided into two parts, the right and the left. The first part, or *Right Ginza*, contains cosmogonies, legends of creation, prayers, and mythology. The second part, or *Left Ginza*, is written upside down and deals exclusively with the dead.

30. Buckley, "With the Mandaeans in Iran," 8.

INTRODUCTION

Though the Mandaeans are a small part of the total population of unreached peoples throughout the world, Christians are commanded to bring the gospel to *every* nation (emphasis added) (Matt 28:19). Given the unprecedented opportunity to reach Mandaean refugees, the more we can understand about their culture and their belief system, the greater the possibility of reaching them with the gospel. The greatest challenge in the past has been the physical inaccessibility of this people group. With the current Diaspora, the physical barriers that have existed in the Middle East are eliminated, at least momentarily. The window of opportunity to reach the unreached Mandaeans is open now and presents opportunities to bring the gospel to them. Using this circumstance wisely will enable the Mandaeans to be among the multitudes surrounding the throne of the King (Rev 7:9).

IMPORTANCE OF PROBLEM

Reaching every nation with the gospel is the mandate of Jesus to his followers (Matt 28:19). Therefore, the unique opportunity to reach a people group that has been formerly unreachable for geographical and philosophical reasons makes this quest of extreme importance. Additionally, the dispersion of Mandaeans throughout the world makes the opportunity even more urgent. They themselves are in a unique position to evangelize other Iraqis, Iranians, and especially other Mandaeans. Therefore, the modest population numbers must be viewed in light of the potential represented by this people group to reach others from the cultures of the Middle East and the Persian culture of Iran.

POSITION ON THE PROBLEM

The assumption of this book is that the Mandaeans, as refugees, are in a unique position to receive the gospel message.[31] Their situation of dislocation and dispersion as refugees and the disruption of their previously closed community, while lamentable in itself, may have a positive result in that it tends to make them more sensitive to spiritual truths. By equipping Christians with current, reliable information, access to the Mandaean

31. This is particularly true in their initial state of being in "limbo," not really knowing where or when they will be resettled, still grieving over the loss of their native home and surroundings. Once they are resettled, they often become more complacent spiritually, reverting to prior practices and beliefs.

refugees with the gospel message tailored to their needs and philosophical viewpoint will be enhanced.

LIMITATIONS

The Mandaeans are a gnostic sect, originating in the early centuries after the ascension of Christ. There are extensive writings on Gnosticism, and the literature about the Mandaeans is growing continually. In spite of this, there is little first-hand knowledge of this people group, save the extensive research done by Lady Drower in the 1940s and by Buckley in the last thirty years. Of particular interest is noted scholar J. J. Buckley's latest book, *Mandaeans: Ancient Texts and Modern People,* in which she describes her visits with Mandaeans in Iraq and in America. From the viewpoint of those sympathetic to the Mandaean plight, however, the academic inquiries may not have been helpful. "Academics interested in the Mandaeans already to some extent treat them as a subject of historic study and do very little to help save the small faith community" from extinction.[32] When Buckley visited Iran, one of the Mandaeans thanked her for telling Muslim scholars and students about Mandaeans and their plight. "His statement says something about the responsibilities of a scholar to a people beset by internal and external perils and astonished that any outsider knows about them at all."[33]

From a Christian missiological perspective, none of these writings answer the question of how to present an opportunity to Mandaean people to know the one truth, Jesus Christ. While serious scholarly efforts have been devoted to uncovering their origin, the date of origin, the location of origin, and their belief systems and rituals, no sources have evaluated the opportunities for the gospel created by the Mandaeans' status as refugees and their dispersion throughout the world. The literature is either completely objective in its intensive academic investigation to uncover various elements of this secret belief system, or it is clearly enamored by the idea of understanding the only remaining gnostic sect.

---

32. Reinke, "Mandaeans in Iraq," 8.
33. Buckley, "With the Mandaeans in Iran," 8.

INTRODUCTION

METHODOLOGY

Descriptive information will be presented to explain the beliefs, history, and current situation of the Mandaeans. The extensive literature available has been evaluated related to the origins, beliefs, and practices of the Mandaeans. However, for purposes of this examination, the literature is somewhat limited due to its focus and perspective on the ancient religion compared with current beliefs and practice. Literature regarding refugees and their inclination to the gospel message has also been reviewed. Additionally, and most importantly, information suited to the purpose of this inquiry has been discovered in consultation with current missionaries and in interviews with Mandaeans who are refugees or have emigrated from Iraq and Iran to the European Union (EU) and North America. Comparative charts, delineating similarities and differences between the Mandaean beliefs and practices and other religions, enhance and clarify information regarding this sect. Understanding the emotional needs of the Iraqi Mandaean refugee, particularly from the context of an exclusivistic, isolationist community, will assist in meeting their physical and emotional needs while seeking opportunities to meet their spiritual needs.

CONCLUSION

Though their numbers are small, it is imperative to see the Mandaeans as among those for whom Christ died. Their presence in Jordan as refugees from Iraq, in the European Union as refugees from Iran, and their dispersion throughout the world, make them more accessible and inclined to the gospel. The breakup of their community, the lack of access to flowing water and priests for baptism, and their predisposition to some tenets similar to Christianity, such as baptism and the return of the judge at the end of the age, afford bridges of opportunity to discuss spiritual matters. The physical movement of Mandaeans from their centuries-old habitat has exposed them to new and different things. This has resulted in the accusation by Iranian Mandaeans that the Iraqi Mandaeans are "suspected of relaxing the rules, more susceptible to modern, secular ideas."[34] It is true that exposure to new information may have the effect of changing their viewpoints and their beliefs. This is especially true of those who are refugees. Having felt the love of Christ through Christians who have assisted in their journey to freedom has resulted in conversions from true darkness to true light. Thus, the unique opportunity presented by the current Diaspora of Mandaeans should not be ignored, but pursued with diligence, integrity, and urgency.

---

34. Buckley, *The Mandaeans*, 66.

2

History and Sources: Gnosticism

INTRODUCTION

GNOSTICISM IS THE PARENT philosophy of Mandaeism. Thus, understanding Mandaeism is enhanced by studying the history and sources that contributed to its development. Gnosticism is generally considered to be one among many false doctrines that the early Christians faced in the centuries after Christ. However, it is not a single entity with clearly defined beliefs. Since about the fourth century, the issue of Gnosticism has lain dormant. Beginning in the nineteenth century, stimulated by the interest of the History of Religions School in Germany, research of Gnosticism became in vogue and several controversies emerged as a result.

The School promulgated "Gnosticism as a discrete religion, older than Christianity and surviving among the Mandaeans of modern times."[1] They saw it as a "pre-Christian phenomenon with its roots in the Orient."[2] Buckley claims that the term Gnosticism "indeed, starts to look very much like a predominantly German invention, an unwieldy creature squeezed into rigid analytical systems."[3]

The discovery of the Nag Hammadi Codices in 1945–46 intensified speculation regarding this belief system, as scholars had attempted—and continue to attempt—to identify Gnosticism's origin, define its characteristics, and uncover its relationship with Christianity, Judaism, Islam, and other Near Eastern and Eastern Religions. However, it does not appear that much

---

1. Edwards, review of *What is Gnosticism?* by Karen L. King, 198.
2. Gilhus, review of *What is Gnosticism?* by Karen L. King, 211.
3. Buckley, review of *What is Gnosticism?* by Karen L. King, 547.

light has been shed on the subject, and these fifty-odd manuscripts clearly "do not fit habitual categories."[4] "After 1,600 years of silence the gnostics finally speak back. Alas, they do not speak with one tongue, but with several, and they say almost nothing about who they were."[5] Rather than answering questions, the "texts instead present a new problem—a complex variety of theological orientations, none orthodox and yet many not quite Gnostic."[6]

Karen L. King, author of *What is Gnosticism?*, provides an in-depth look at the history and development of this belief system in the twentieth century. She contends that there is no such thing as Gnosticism, in spite of the Nag Hammadi discovery, and she goes to great lengths to urge abolishment of the term in scholarly circles. King apparently disagrees with scholars who believe that the Nag Hammadi Codices have indeed provided evidence of a "belief system with its own prayers, creeds, and worship."[7] That "the discovery of the Nag Hammadi Library casts new light on the questions of definition and Gnostic origins" was the theme of the 1983 Springfield Seminar.[8] The 1945 discovery provided new source material, but also raised new questions. The historical period of these manuscripts has been determined ca. 350 CE, but the users of these documents are still a mystery; though the dating of individual texts is unknown, the papyrus manuscripts are from the mid-fourth century CE. And because the find contains manuscripts with no evidence of Christian influence,

> it demonstrates beyond question that gnosticism was not simply a Christian heresy. . . . While there may be no extant Gnostic manuscripts from the early first century CE to show that there existed a pre-Christian gnosticism in a *chronological* sense, these texts clearly demonstrate the existence of pre-Christian gnosticism in an *ideological* sense. Such hard evidence presents a previously unavailable avenue for investigating the interaction between Christianity and its Gnostic opponents.[9]

---

4. Ibid., 548.

5. Gilhus, review of *What is Gnosticism?* by Karen L. King, 212.

6. Mirecki, review of *What is Gnosticism?* by Karen L. King, 350.

7. Rorem, review of *Hag Hammadi, Gnosticism, and Early Christianity*, Charles W Hedrick and Robert Hodgson, Jr, eds., 286.

8. Hedrick and Hodgson, Jr. eds., *Nag Hammadi, Gnosticism, and Early Christianity*, 4–5; The 1983 Springfield, Missouri Working Seminar on Gnosticism and Early Christianity, March 30–April 2, 1983, concentrated exclusively on the relationship between Gnosticism and early Christianity, Ibid., 7.

9. Ibid., 8–9.

In contrast, Rudolph claims that "the entire corpus seems to have been collected and used by Christian Gnostics."[10]

Since the first few centuries after Christ, there is no evidence of a legacy of Gnosticism in the world, except for the Mandaeans of Iraq and Iran. It would appear that, "as biblical Christianity was more clearly understood, Gnosticism's inadequacies became more apparent and eventually they yielded to the force of the strong logic which Christian orthodoxy represented."[11] Riemer Roukema, noted author on Gnosticism and its role in early Christian history, "demonstrates that the main Gnostic themes simply could not compete with their orthodox rivals."[12]

CONTROVERSIES ON DEFINITIONS

Defining Gnosticism has been a major challenge in studying this belief system. King argues that Gnosticism is a

> rhetorical term which has been confused with a historical entity. There was and is no such thing as Gnosticism, if we mean by that some kind of ancient religious entity with a single origin and a distinct set of characteristics. . . . The term 'Gnosticism' was first used by Henry More in 1669. . . . The term 'knowledge' is translated from the Greek word *gnosis*, but in Gnosticism it has come to stand for false knowledge, in short, for heresy" [against the Orthodox Church].[13]

Until the twentieth century, scholars seemed to have reached a common understanding of Gnosticism. However, in 1966, a major conclave of international academicians met in Messina, Italy, for the purpose of discovering Gnosticism's origin and defining the essence of Gnosticism in order to align their collective understanding and their individual research. The outcome was there was no clear definition to which they could all agree. The only agreement that came out of that conference was the differentiation between the "general term 'gnosis,' which was taken to mean 'knowledge of the divine mysteries reserved for an elite,' and 'gnosticism,' which was applied to a more specific assortment of religious systems or sects who

---

10. Rudolph, "Gnosticism," 191.
11. Bray, review of *Gnosis and Faith in Early Christianity*, by Riemer Roukema, 93.
12. Ibid., 93.
13. King, *What Is Gnosticism?* 1, 7.

are historically attested beginning in the second century CE."[14] Yamauchi believes that those who define Gnosticism very narrowly "do not find conclusive evidence of pre-Christian Gnosticism, whereas those scholars who operate with a 'broad' definition of Gnosticism find it not only in the New Testament but in many other early documents as well."[15]

As a result of this lack of definition, several scholars, notably Karen L. King and Michael A. Williams, have suggested the category called "Gnosticism" is misleading and should be abandoned. While King "encourages us to hear differing voices . . . (she) leaves us with more questions than answers."[16] Williams suggests replacing the term Gnosticism with the alternative phrase "biblical demiurgical traditions," to make a distinction from those gnostic traditions that ascribe creation and management of the cosmos to a lower entity (demiurge) distinct from the highest God, as in Platonism. Williams narrows the category of Gnosticism considerably with the addition of the "adjective 'biblical,' to denote 'demiurgical' traditions that also incorporate or adapt traditions from Jewish or Christian Scripture."[17]

CONTROVERSIES ON THE ORIGIN OF GNOSTICISM

The early church fathers identified Simon Magus of Samaria (Acts 8) as the originator of Gnosticism.[18] Irenaeus alleged that Simon was "the one from whom all heresies originated."[19] Some sources agree that "as a definite entity Gnosticism appears with Simon Magus (and others) and it appears in an entirely Jewish and Christian context."[20] It is argued that since the formation of Christianity's identity was woven into the apologetics and polemics of these early centuries, the early church tended to identify beliefs in conflict with the church's position as heresy, often placing them in the still ill-defined category of "Gnosticism." However, Smith provides an extensive survey of the issues surrounding the rise of Gnosticism and argues with considerable confidence that "there is little evidence that supports this

14. Williams, *Rethinking "Gnosticism,"* 27.
15. Yamauchi, *Pre-Christian Gnosticism*, 13–14.
16. McCarthy, review of *What is Gnosticism?*, 640.
17. Williams, *Rethinking "Gnosticism,"* 51.
18. Smith, *No Longer Jews*, 3.
19. Coxe, *Ante-Nicene Fathers*, 347–48.
20. Mead, *Gnostics*, xv.

claim or even identifies Simon as Gnostic," particularly in light of it being "a well-established fact that the Christian apologists of the second century were not accurate historians."[21]

Most scholars agree Gnosticism did not originate from a single source. In fact, the literature identifies the influence of many belief systems on Gnosticism's development. Smith agrees Gnosticism "has affinities with themes from many religions of the ancient world, but none of them provide the innovation that became Gnosticism in the second century."[22] He argues that Gnosticism developed when "the three streams of Judaism, Christianity, and Platonism converge(d), obviously with varying degrees of emphasis, with anti-Judaism being a crucial feature."[23] The "anti-Judaism" element that is essential to Gnosticism, as articulated by Basilides of Egypt, is the devolution of the God of the Old Testament to an evil demiurge who created the world in opposition to the supreme God.[24] The Christian element essential to Gnosticism is the "redeemer" who comes to inform humans of their innate deity, having had a spark of divinity implanted in them. The platonic elements of Gnosticism are anti-cosmic dualism and mythology. Smith's position is that it was the "ripe intellectual and historical (and perhaps geographical) context in which the innovation of Gnosticism could have occurred, resulting in the creative Gnostic religion of the early second century CE"[25]

Some scholars assert it was "out of the melting pot of religions that was Palestine at the beginning of the Christian era, that Gnosticism arose."[26] However, with considerable evidence, Smith's extensive evaluation considers Egypt as an attractive hypothesis as Gnosticism's place of origin, based on "the fact that the first historically viable Gnostics came from Egypt: Basilides, Carpocrates and his libertine son, Epiphanes and Valentinus," and Egypt is where "all the chief elements integral to the Gnostic systems were present."[27]

21. Smith, *No Longer Jews*, 3.
22. Ibid., 19.
23. Ibid., 250.
24. Ibid., 2–3.
25. Ibid., 18.
26. Mead, *Gnostics*, xvi.
27. Smith, *No Longer Jews*, 3, 251.

CONTROVERSIES ON THE CHARACTERISTICS OF GNOSTICISM

No gnostic text or belief system reflects all of the characteristics that have been identified, nor are they reflected uniformly or equally if they are present. Additionally, many gnostic elements can be seen in other religious and philosophical systems of the ancient world. With these caveats in mind, the primary characteristics of Gnosticism are:

A Supreme Being or *Absolute Sovereign* is transcendent over all, beyond human understanding and comprehension, yet "invariably good.... Nearly always evil is inherent in matter in the manner of a physical quality."[28] This transcendent god is the source of "knowledge which alone can save."[29]

Creation was accomplished by a lesser god in rebellion against the Supreme Being. The world is generally regarded from a pessimistic viewpoint. Thus, all that was created—matter—is evil. When the Supreme Being saw what the underling, or demiurge, had done, he determined that humans were at least eligible to be returned to their heavenly origin, so he deposited a spark of divinity in each person. The "divine spark" theory can be traced back to the Stoics.[30] In Gnosticism, the creation myth is "anti-Jewish, or anti-Creator—that is anti-'the God of the Old Testament.' Through some means, gnostics came to identify the God of the Jews as inferior to and separate from the true and highest God, and they defined the product of his creative activity as evil."[31]

Roukema describes in detail the devastating results of this type of thinking on the early Christian church, as he commends the church fathers for their wisdom in declaring these beliefs heresy. The gnostic distinction between a higher good god as the father and a lower god as the creator was countered by Irenaeus' argument that there is one God who has made all, visible and invisible, through his Word, Jesus Christ, who is also the redeemer. This means the God of the Old Testament is the same as the God of the New Testament. This gives credibility to the redeemer, Jesus (who therefore was God of the earth as well as the heavens), and the physical resurrection of the dead. Roukema concludes with perhaps the most important benefit of the church fathers' decision regarding the unity of God:

---

28. Yamauchi, *Pre-Christian Gnosticism*, 14.
29. Wilson, *Gnostic Problem*, 70.
30. Ibid., 69.
31. Smith, *No Longer Jews*, 2.

If the church had gone along with it (the splitting of the God of the OT and the NT), then the bond with the people of Israel would have been cut more than ever. The God of the Jewish people would then have been different from the Father by whom Jesus Christ knew he had been sent. Jesus would then not stand in the line of the Old Testament prophets, but would have proclaimed a completely new, heavenly message. . . . [In preserving] the Old Testament as holy Scripture for the Church . . . they made it clear that the Christian faith stems from God who has created life on earth and who has started on a history with humankind from the beginning. . . . By starting from the Old Testament, Christian faith opposes the feeling that gnosticism causes, namely that life on earth is profoundly meaningless or serves only a heavenly purpose."[32]

Gnosis, the ability to "know," was implanted as part of this spark of divinity, creating within each human the desire and ability to know the secrets of the divine. Gnosis, or knowledge, is the key to salvation, rather than faith or obedience to laws. Thus, humans would come to realize their true place in the heavenlies and would eventually arrive back at their destiny after earthly death. "The saving 'knowledge' involves a revelation as to the true nature both of the self and of God; indeed, for the Gnostic, self-knowledge *is* knowledge of God."[33] This gnosis or knowledge is "given by revelation, which has been made available only to the elect who are capable of receiving it, and therefore (it) has an esoteric character."[34] This notion of elitism has since been challenged by Roukema, who asserts that "Gnostics were ready to share their special gnosis with others or saw this as their task. Nor did they always think that they alone had a share in redemption."[35] However, the demise of the gnostic belief indicates that minimal missionary effort occurred at their behest. Additionally, the only surviving gnostic belief system, the Mandaeans, is very secretive and definitely does not see others outside their own sect as being capable or worthy of receiving redemption. This lends support to the notion that sharing gnosis was not a widespread practice.

A *Redeemer*, a representative of the Supreme Being who is unknowable and unapproachable, is the rescuer of humans, and directs or guides them back into the heavenlies, along with aeons, who, depending on the myth under consideration, either escort the soul or test it along the way. The human

32. Roukema, *Gnosis and Faith*, 160–61.
33. Smith, *No Longer Jews*, 11.
34. Rudolph, *Gnosis*, 55.
35. Roukema, *Gnosis and Faith*, 168.

soul must be redeemed from the portion of humanity that is the prison of the soul, the human body. "In Oriental religions, redeemers somewhat analogous to the Gnostic ones may have existed, but thus far no one has been able to prove that they were known as such before the rise of Gnostic thought.... The most obvious explanation of the origin of the Gnostic redeemer is that he was modeled [sic] after the Christian conception of Jesus."[36] Further, the redeemer is often seen as a redeemed redeemer, a phenomenon that some have tried to attribute to pre-Christian Gnosticism. However, Yamauchi argues effectively against a pre-Christian redeemer, demonstrating that the leading scholars have come to deny a pre-Christian Redeemer myth and concluding that such a myth is generally rejected.[37]

However, since not all of these characteristics are found in all gnostic systems, there are "systems without a redeemer myth ... [that] appear frequently among the early accounts of Jewish and Christian Gnosticism ... [including] the original systems of the Naassenes, the Valentinians and the Marcosians."[38]

Dualism is a basic foundation in Gnosticism, pitting spirit as good against matter as evil. This is considered by some as the most unique and definitive element of Gnosticism as many of the other components can be traced to other belief systems.[39] "Ethical dualism" of light versus darkness is common to other religions of the Near East, but the "dualism unique to the gnostics identifies the spiritual realm of nature and the universe as morally good and the physical domain as evil, not merely less good as in various Platonic systems."[40]

Eschatology or *Last Things* is the final restoration of the soul to heaven, of not only individuals at their earthly, physical death, but of all of the "elect" when the material world comes to an end.

Mythology is the glue that holds everything together for the gnostic. There is an elaborate mythical system by which gnostics understand their

---

36. Grant, *Gnosticism*, 18.

37. Yamauchi, *Pre-Christian Gnosticism*, 15, 29–30, 165–66. The legend of a redeemed redeemer asserts that a redeemer is sent from heaven to alert man of his divine origin and gives man the gnosis to bring man back into his divine state. The redeemer then re-ascends to heaven, defeating demonic powers along the way, thus preparing the path for those who will follow. As the souls of man are re-gathered in heaven, the Redeemer is himself redeemed.

38. Schmithals, *Gnosticism in Corinth*, 45.

39. Smith, *No Longer Jews*, 1.

40. Ibid., 2.

universe and their place in it. They see themselves as a part of the heavenly divinity, assigned to earth for a period of time, but destined to return to their heavenly origins upon death.

Cult and Community involves a fair amount of speculation since we know very little about it. However, it is included because it is a critical element among the Mandaeans, which is the only gnostic sect remaining. It may be seriously contended that the reason for their survival has been their tight-knit, secretive, exclusivistic community, which until the late 1990s has been able to exist and thrive in spite of the pressures of the world around them.

Syncretism, also called *Parasitism*, is the precise problem in defining the relationship of Gnosticism with other Near Eastern religions, especially Judaism and early Christianity.[41] Gnosticism had the unique ability to innovate its beliefs based upon new revelations, which often reflected the landscape in which it was immersed. It had no traditions of its own, only those that were borrowed from other religions. There appears to be no exclusivity between the different branches of Gnosticism, nor did they have their own canon of scripture, unless it was that of other religions, which they employed and interpreted for their own purposes. They became masters at "extracting as much as possible out of the thoughts and expressing it in ever new ways. . . . (Thus) a statement of the text was given a deeper meaning, or even several, in order to claim it for one's own doctrine or to display its inner richness."[42]

However, Hedrick presents a contrary view from his analysis of the nature of the gnostic manuscripts from the Nag Hammadi findings. While most of the academic literature supports the notion of generally harmonious gnostic groups, united in their opposition to Christianity, Hedrick asserts they were in competition with one another as well.[43]

CONCLUSION

It is readily observed that controversy within the study of Gnosticism is deep and broad, as is the study of Mandaeism. There seems to be no element of this belief system about which scholars completely agree.

---

41. Ibid., 12.
42. Rudolph, *Gnosis*, 54.
43. Hedrick and Hodgson, Jr. eds., *Nag Hammadi, Gnosticism, and Early Christianity*, 10.

However, based upon the information available at this time, it seems the gnostic belief system is the antithesis of the Christian belief system. While both systems view the Supreme Being, God, as good, the gnostic system cannot explain evil except by creating a different and distinct deity. While both systems recognize the Supreme Being as omniscient, the gnostic system considers omniscience as something humans can achieve. While both systems generally recognize a redeemer, the gnostic system believes redemption is achieved through human effort, perhaps with some assistance or guidance from the redeemer. While both systems believe in an after-life, the gnostic system believes that the soul is inherently part of God and will be reunited as part of deity in the end. While both systems believe the world as we know it will end, the gnostic system believes this will signal the end of matter, which is evil. While both systems recognize the difference between good and evil, or light and darkness, the gnostic system assigns a physical characteristic, matter, to the evil or dark elements, failing to recognize the spiritual elements of evil and darkness.

While it is of interest to compare, contrast, and investigate the belief systems of ages past, one must be aware of Paul's warning to the Colossians to "beware of philosophy" (Col 2:8). In a fascinating article warning Christian scholars and philosophers to beware of philosophy, Norman L. Geisler describes the inherent philosophies that stem from man's imagination.[44] He shows how the presuppositions of scholars through the ages have resulted in the denial of miracles and predictive prophecy, and have turned the gospel history into religious mythology. By applying the naturalistic methodology of philosophy to science, society, and religion, the widespread notion that evolution is scientifically proven has resulted, along with the idea that religion has evolved from magic to polytheism to monotheism to the atheism we know today.

Paul's exhortation to the Corinthians, along this same line, is that though "I can fathom all mysteries and all knowledge . . . but have not love, I am nothing" (1 Cor 13:2). Geisler's admonition to scholars and philosophers is to be aware that those investigating philosophies must be aware that it is in the realm of spiritual warfare, and that the temptation of those investigating must be tempered by precautions against false ideology and their adherence to the Lordship of Christ over scholarship. He argues that

---

44. Geisler, "Beware of Philosophy," 15.

"Scholarship should be used to build Christ's spiritual kingdom, not to build an academic kingdom for one's self."[45]

Irenaeus is recognized as perhaps the most effective and prolific polemicist against Gnosticism. Edwards points out, however, it was not his intent to portray Gnosticism as a specific or uniform belief system that opposed Christianity. Rather, it was Irenaeus' argument

> that truth is one while error is various, and the only trait that (the followers of these heresies) . . . have in common is that all make a presumptuous claim to *gnosis*, that is to knowledge acquired through personal revelation or private judgment without the guidance of the Church. He does not pretend that every professor of gnosis claimed the same knowledge, let alone that everyone styled himself a *gnostickos* . . .[46]

Thus, while critics claim the church fathers smothered an ancient belief system, we can be thankful it was through God and his people that such notions were put to rest in the early centuries after Christ. This author agrees with Roukema, who concludes that Gnosticism was rightly rejected by the Church fathers, based on three facts. "First, it was disastrous to separate the God of Jesus from the God of the OT. Second, it was historically mistaken to suggest that Jesus came with a special *gnosis* for the elect. Third, it was elitist, believing that they alone had the *gnosis* and hence salvation."[47]

---

45. Ibid., 15.

46. Edwards, Review of *What is Gnosticism?*, by Karen L. King, 199.

47. Moyise, Review of *Gnosis and Faith in Early Christianity*, by Riemer Roukema, 328.

3

History and Sources: Mandaeism

INTRODUCTION

MANDAEISM NOT ONLY SHARES remarkable similarities to gnostic beliefs. It "adheres to the typical Gnostic doctrines and mythologies regarding the soul's entrapment in earthly life and the existence of a heavenly Lightworld, the soul's true home."[1] It also shares a "similar mode of expression, through myth. In other words, we do not find philosophical reflections but stories."[2] In fact, it is impossible to reconstruct a unified, coherent vision of certain important aspects of religious doctrine because of the different Mandaean teachings recorded centuries apart. "Mandaean literature is confused and self-contradictory . . . [consisting] of many parts which belong to different historical periods and contain[ing] both old and new elements."[3] "The more ancient traditions seem clearly dualistic and are nearest to the ideal positions of classical Gnosticism. There are also texts, however, where the physical world is seen in a positive light, considered the direct creation of the highest, good divinity. These passages must have been redacted in periods of clear cultural dependence on Christianity, or perhaps on Islam."[4] In fact, the *Ginza*, the Mandaean holy book, describes seven different accounts of the origins of the cosmos, each "with features that are most difficult to reconcile."[5] This conflict is also evident among the individuals

---

1. Buckley, "With the Mandaeans in Iran," 8.
2. Lupieri, *The Mandaeans*, 38.
3. Gunduz, "The Problems of the Nature and Date of Mandaean Sources," 89.
4. Lupieri, *The Mandaeans*, 38.
5. Ibid., 38.

who conveyed information to various scholars throughout the past centuries. Since each Mandaean is endowed with certain revelation or truth that others may not possess, the truth one knows may conflict with the truth others in the sect have. The way this conflict is overcome is to recognize that all truth is secret, and thus, a reluctance or inability to communicate it is part of the complexity of this religion. Lady Drower found this inconsistency in the written *Ginza* and the information communicated to her by trusted informants from the priestly caste. These discrepancies are still experienced today by practicing Mandaeans and are simply accepted as the fact that each person may have different truths or different levels of the same truths. This demonstrates the essence of Mandaeism's syncretism; it simply incorporates all beliefs into its system as truth and "does not seem to have developed a theological orthodoxy capable of pushing dissident opinion aside."[6] Buckley asserts that "such dynamics demonstrate that the religion remains in conversation with itself, and these debates should not be interpreted as glaring contradictions, hopeless fragmentation, or loss of identity."[7] Indeed, this dynamism stems from the fact that many of the Mandaean mythological figures "travel between realms, [are] hard to pin down, [and] resistant to stasis."[8]

THE GNOSTIC ELEMENTS OF MANDAEISM

All of the nine attributes of Gnosticism listed in chapter 2 are present in the Mandaean belief system. Perhaps the predominant feature of Gnosticism in Mandaeism is its syncretism, its ability to reinvent itself based on new information or influences. That this strain of Gnosticism has survived until the twenty-first century is often attributed to Mandaeism's unique ability to incorporate other beliefs and practices into its system.

The Supreme Being in Mandaeism is called by different names, including the Great Life or First Life, *Mara d-Rabuta* (Lord of Greatness); *Malka d-Nhura* (King of Light, First Light), and *Mana* (Powerful). The First Life does not travel or maintain contact with humans, but sits above all, overseeing everything. He presides at the pinnacle of the Lightworld, majestically enthroned, the royal chief of the saving ambassador *utras* and of all Mandaeans. He is the good spirit who reigns supreme over all. From this

6. Ibid., 39.
7. Buckley, *The Mandaeans*, 7.
8. Ibid., 35.

First Light emanates the Second Light, whose name is derived from the secret name of Yahweh, but whose position in the Mandaean pantheon is ambiguous.[9] The Third Light is called *Abatur*, who is the judge at the end of time, and the Fourth Light is *Ptahil*, who is the least perfect and is found at the edge of light, in contact with darkness.

There are a number of celestial beings, called *utria*. These beings are intermediaries and messengers between humans and the First Being, and thus were identified as angels by missionaries of past centuries. *Manda d-Hiia*, Knowledge of Life, is the preeminent *utra*. He is often equated with Jesus of Christianity.

The *creators* of the cosmos are *Yasamin*, who is a prototype of a Mandaean priest who suffers from excessive pride; *Abatur*, who is the judge; and *Ptahil*, who is under the orders of his father, *Abatur*. All three have complex double personalities, which may be negative or positive depending on the circumstances. These three are also portrayed as saviors in other settings. *Abatur*, the "guardian of the scales" and the judge at the end of time, detests this role, which is punishment for his involvement in the creation by insufficiently training his son *Ptahil*.[10] Though this role as judge might seem a powerful and important role, "in the Mandaean view, Abatur's position is a form of punishment, a thankless, contemptible task."[11]

Creation is portrayed by a number of different descriptions. These are generally divided between the eternal existence of two oppositional worlds, the Lightworld and the world of darkness, and the emanation model, described above, which is more common. Moreover, the "sheer mass of variations in their creation mythology makes it impossible to appoint one specific version as 'the original'."[12]

Gnosis, the ability to "know," was implanted as a spark of divinity, creating within each Mandaean the desire and ability to know the secrets of the divine. When man was created, the First Life endowed humans with the ability to know all things. These things are secret, revealed over time to individuals and passed on as other individuals are fit to receive that knowledge. Mandaeism is defined as "self-designated 'knowers.'"[13] The people are

---

9. Lupieri, *The Mandaeans*, 39. This secret name of Yahweh, Iao, is present in numerous magic and gnostic texts and is generally considered a positive divinity.
10. Buckley, *The Mandaeans*, 38.
11. Ibid., 38.
12. Ibid., 8.
13. Ibid., 7.

History and Sources: Mandaeism

secretive and defensive about their beliefs and practices. Marriage outside the sect is not allowed, nor are conversions into the sect. Knowledge is reserved for the leaders and careful attention to their lineage is preserved.

However, even those born into this sect often do not have much information about their actual beliefs. It is primarily the responsibility of the family to teach the beliefs. However, they are at a disadvantage since knowledge is dispensed only by the priests. Mandaeism is seen as "an absolutely exceptional religion . . . [having been] preserved by a small nucleus of believers who are socially discriminated against and immersed in a hostile ethno-religious context."[14] Its secret knowledge is reserved for a tiny minority and thus "has exposed the group to constant danger through biological extinction of the caste invested with this knowledge."[15] Thus, it has often had to camouflage itself in its surrounding religious world. "The people are at a disadvantage because they don't know their beliefs, relying on the clerics to decide everything for them. Yet, they are afraid to leave since they only have a single frame of reference and to leave their tradition is frightening."[16]

The *redeemer* is represented primarily by *Hibil*, also called *Hibil Ziwa*, who is part of the trinity of Mandaeism. All three members of this triumvirate can substitute for *Manda d-Hiia* as revealers and are also saviors or redeemers, depending on the circumstances. A recurring formula in Mandaean prayers is "In the name of *Hibil*, *Sitil* and *Anus*."[17] These three are brothers from different generations. *Hibil*, who is Abel in his human form, is the savior. *Hibil Ziwa* follows the gnostic patterns of the descent of the heavenly savior into the darkness, ultimately needing to be freed by divine intervention. "In short, *Hibil Ziwa* impersonates the so-called 'savior to be saved,' very much a part of Gnostic tradition."[18] In legends, he is referred to interchangeably with *Manda d-Hiia* as revealer. He also appears in a creation myth as the creator.

Sitil, called Seth in his humanity, is pure. He has never slept with a woman, is innocent of bloodshed and agreed to die instead of his father, Adam. He is virtually sinless, in his humanity.[19] According to legend, *Abatur* compares each person's purity after death against *Sitil's* purity to determine the degree

---

14. Lupieri, *The Mandaeans*, xviii.
15. Ibid., xviii.
16. Bejjani, discussion with author, 7 Mar 2005 and 27 Feb 2006.
17. Buckley, *The Mandaeans*, 35.
18. Lupieri, *The Mandaeans*, 48.
19. Buckley, *The Mandaeans*, 36–38.

of his punishment on his ascent to the Lightworld. Because of *Sitil's* untimely death, before his father Adam who refused to die, *Sitil* reversed the expected pattern of parents dying before children and he became the first death. "*Sitil's* purity above all other humans is ensured because he died instead of his father."[20] He is the first human death and the first to ascend to the Lightworld from earth. Because of his purity, he was immediately elevated from humanity to the status of celestial being, an *utra*.

Anus is a healer and preacher whose role resembles that of Jesus. *Anus* is described in legend as coming to Jerusalem in bodily form, where he

> heals the sick, makes the blind see, purifies the lepers, makes the cripples that drag themselves along the ground walk straight, makes the deaf-mutes talk and gives life to the dead. He identifies the faithful among the Jews and instructs them: 'There is death and there is life; there is darkness and there is light; there is error and there is truth.' He calls upon the Jews to convert in the name of the Most High King of light."[21]

The *Left Ginza* presents another, unnamed savior, who "not only informs the soul of its heavenly origin, [but] he returns at the death of the particular person and at the end of the world, to lead the individual and the world soul upward to its home. . . . [This being] is related to the soul in a peculiar manner . . . where the messenger and soul are the two manifestations of the one divided personality."[22]

Dualism is an important aspect of Mandaeism. The world is seen as opposing and conflicting principles. There is

> division between good and evil on earth (ethical dualism), the forces of good and evil, of light and darkness battle throughout the entire universe (cosmic dualism). Even divinity is divided . . . (this dualistic vision of the divine is tempered) with the idea that in the beginning there was only one positive divine principle, the Light, which later degenerated through multiple emanations until the last of these got caught up in matter, conceived of as negativity, void, and absence.[23]

---

20. Ibid., 36.
21. Lupieri, *The Mandaeans*, 244.
22. Kraeling, *Anthropos*, 68–69.
23. Lupieri, *The Mandaeans*, 37.

History and Sources: Mandaeism

The imbalance between the negative and positive, which led to the origin of this world, "will cease only when the irreconcilable components of the cosmos, once again completely separated with the light that is dispersed and imprisoned in darkness, has been recovered in all its parts, and return(s) to the enjoyment of an eternal equilibrium."[24] In common with other gnostic systems, Mandaeism sees "human beings living in fundamental alienation on earth while the true home lies up above, in the light."[25]

Eschatology represents one of the syncretistic features of the Mandaean doctrine in the "parallel nature of the figures of *Manda d-Hiia* and Jesus Christ, considering the former a derivation of the latter."[26] The signs that Christians point to indicating the imminent return of Jesus are the same signs that Mandaeans point to indicating the coming of their messiah. One of the main indicators of the coming of their messiah is that Mandaeans will begin leaving their faith, converting to other religions. This is happening frequently and is considered a sign that the end will soon come. At that time, all the Mandaeans will go directly to the Lightworld from earth. Some Mandaean texts indicate Jesus will return to earth; others indicate that *Anus* or *Manda d-Hiia* will return.[27] Finally, they believe in a final judgment of all people by the judge, *Abatur*, and the final destruction of earth. When all the Mandaeans are taken to the Lightworld from earth, the earth will be destroyed.

Mythology is prominent in Mandaean beliefs. In addition to sharing similar gnostic elements, Mandaeism shares the gnostic mode of expression of its beliefs through mythology and legends. Legends about Mary, Jesus' mother, John the Baptist, and many of the Old Testament characters are part of the fabric of this belief system. Mandaeism has its own mythological system, an enormous body of literature that spans a number of genres and has rarely been studied in modern times. Its lengthy and detailed rituals resist easy interpretation. One of the most difficult aspects of researching the Mandaeans is the ambiguity regarding every aspect of the character of this sect. As illustrated above, there are various myths describing creation, as well as the end of time. It is difficult to categorize their beliefs with clarity "into an overall scheme respecting our normal canons of logic. Our own

---

24. Ibid., 38.
25. Buckley, *The Mandaeans*, 7.
26. Lupieri, *The Mandaeans*, 116.
27. Ibid., 52.

logic in fact does not seem to be the ideal means to reach an understanding of Mandaean traditions."[28]

Cult and Community are extremely strong in the Mandaean culture. The practices of the faith are predominant in their daily lives and the community is reinforced by keeping track of blood lines (for those aspiring to the priesthood), marriage within the community, prohibition from conversion into the sect, and separation from the world around them.

Especially important are Mandaean holidays honoring their ancestors. These holidays always include particular foods, baptisms, and prayers for those who have gone on before.

Although the Diaspora has fractured the community, creative technological efforts are underway to keep them connected throughout the world. This is described in more detail in chapter 4.

Syncretism is a most striking element of Mandaeism. The sect has created and reinvented its beliefs according to external influences. This is the primary topic of this chapter, as we discover the elements of Judaism, Christianity, and Islam that have become a part of Mandaeism. Table 1 compares the major beliefs of Mandaeism and Gnosticism.

28. Ibid., 52.

Table 1. Mandaeism vis-à-vis Gnosticism

Belief	Mandaeism	Gnosticism
Supreme Being, transcendent over all	This being is good; no evil in him; no contact with humans.	This being is good; no evil in him.
Creation	Many different and conflicting legends; two main themes are creation as a result of darkness against the light (two separate and warring entities), or the emanation model, in which sparks of divinity emanated from the Supreme Being into the Mandaeans.	Accomplished by a lesser god; the Supreme Being implanted a spark of divinity in each person.
Gnosis (Knowledge)	Gnosis was implanted as part of this spark of divinity. Gnosis is the key to salvation. However, it is reserved to Mandaeans, and specifically to priests. Cannot be shared with outsiders.	Gnosis was implanted as part of this spark of divinity. Gnosis is the key to salvation. Gnosis was encouraged to be shared with others.
Redeemer	This role is played in varying degrees by several of the mythological characters. The primary responsibility of the redeemer-types is to assist Mandaean souls to the Lightworld, as they encounter obstruction along the journey.	A representative of the Supreme Being who rescues and/or guides humans to the heavenlies; some test along the way.
Dualism	Mandaeans see the world as opposing, between good and evil on earth, but also in the entire universe. Even divinity is divided between good and bad. This will be resolved at the end of the world. Mandaeism is opposed to the asceticism and celibacy common in other forms of Gnosticism.	Good is represented in spiritual and evil is represented in matter or physical. This results in asceticism, which regards even the body as repulsive.

The Mandaeans—Baptizers of Iraq and Iran

Belief	Mandaeism	Gnosticism
Eschatology	A being parallel to Jesus (in some texts it is Jesus) will return at the end of the world to escort all Mandaeans to the Lightworld. No other humans will enter heaven except Mandaeans.	Souls are returned to heavenly home at their physical death, and also when the material world comes to an end.
Mythology	Legends and mythology, including mythological characters, explain the universe and all that happens within it. Most of the legends portray characters from the Bible, although in striking dissimilarities to the biblical versions. (Examples include Jesus as false prophet, Abraham as leader of Mandaeans until he succumbed to circumcision, Adam as refusing to die.)	Legends and mythology, including mythological characters, explain the universe and all that happens within it.
Cult and Community	This trait among the Mandaeans may be a primary reason they have survived. As they allow no conversion into the sect, and no marriages outside the sect, they have been able to maintain their autonomy for centuries.	Very little known about ancient Gnostic communities.
Syncretism	Very clear evidence of adopting beliefs of other faiths in order to survive. Called a faith in tension and a belief system in constant communication with itself, it reinvents itself as circumstances require. Have created written liturgy to validate its religious doctrines.	Gnosticism has no traditions of its own; everything within Gnosticism is taken from other religions of the time. There is no canon of scripture.

THE ORIGIN OF MANDAEISM

The origin of the Mandaeans is a question that is fraught with contradictory evidence. The explanation of Mandaean origin and history "is legendary and full of fantasy," often giving conflicting information according to some sources.[29] The Mandaeans claim that their beliefs and religion were formed by Adam. Legend informs us that Adam was given a spark of the divine during his creation. He did not sin in the garden but reaffirmed the right that made him like God by eating the fruit of the tree of knowledge, actually fulfilling his destiny of gaining knowledge. That knowledge was given directly from the First Life and included the method and significance of baptism in order to reunite with the Lightworld. Other information claims that there is no specific founder of Mandaeism, but that Abraham was considered a Mandaean (until he was circumcised) and that John the Baptist was the last messenger to the Mandaeans.[30] The earliest known sacred writings of the Mandaeans are mid-seventh century, produced to prove to the Muslims that they qualified as *ahl al-kitab*.[31]

A dilemma that has plagued researchers of the Mandaeans is the effort to categorize them. From a "dissident Christian sect" to a "splinter group from Hellenistic Judaism" to "the only surviving (from the ancient world) group of Gnostics," there is agreement only on the fact that they cannot be easily classified.[32] Buckley doubts they ever had a Christian stage, asserting that there is a "consensus, based on linguistic and historical research that puts Mandaeism back into its original, 'heretical' Jewish baptist milieu," though she recognizes the "strong anti-Christian as well as anti-Jewish sentiment in Mandaean traditions."[33] Further, Buckley notes the Friday evening prayers, coinciding with the beginning of the Jewish Sabbath, and the Saturday evening prayers, marking the end of Jewish Sabbath, both honor Mary and at the same time are highly polemical in content. These two prayers function as "a weekly restatement of Mandaeism's cut ties to Judaism, as a repeated exorcism."[34] However, Buckley also acknowledges that

---

29. Gunduz, "The Problems of the Nature and Date of Mandaean Sources," 93.

30. Lupieri, *The Mandaeans*, 10.

31. Buckley, *The Mandaeans*, 5; de Blois, "The 'Sabians' in Pre-Islamic Arabia," 40; Buckley, "The Mandaean Appropriation of Jesus' Mother, Miriai," 184.

32. de Blois, "The 'Sabians' in Pre-Islamic Arabia," 44; Cohn-Sherbok, "The Mandaeans and Heterodox Judaism," 148; Buckley, *The Mandaeans*, 7.

33. Buckley, "Jesus' Mother," 181, 183.

34. Ibid., 193.

Mary's "very presence raises the issue of the possibility of a brief, Christian stage in early Mandaeism."[35]

One of the clearest reasons for the syncretization of the Mandaean religion with other religions is their location in the midst of Muslims. Since the seventh century, they have been under the rule of Muslims, and have had to maintain their traditions, and indeed, their viability, under adverse and potentially fatal circumstances. Fortunately, they seized an opportunity in the Qur'an that proved to be their salvation from extinction. The Qur'an provides for *ahl al-kitab*, which acknowledges 'people of the Book,' "people who profess a religion recognized by Islam to have been of divine origin."[36] To be *ahl al-kitab* requires monotheism and a holy, divine book. The Sabians, another name for Mandaeans, are specifically listed in Surahs 2:62, 5:69, and in 22:17, which specifically classify the *ahl al-kitab*. The first two passages

> list four religions: 'those who believe' (evidently meaning the Muslims), the Jews, the Christians and the Sabiun, all of whom, provided they actually fulfill their religious duties, are, or at least were at some time in the past, potential candidates for salvation. As such, they stand in stark contrast to the polytheists, the 'associators', who, the Qur'an insists, are destined to damnation. Although it is nowhere explicitly stated that the Sabiun are 'people of the book'—this designation is expressly applied only to the Jews and Christians—the fact that in these verses they are mentioned together with the Jews and Christians has on the whole led Muslim interpreters to the (plausible) deduction that the Sabiun are in fact *ahl al-kitab*, that is to say that they had a more-or-less monotheistic faith and a book that had been given to them by a genuine god-sent prophet.[37]

Yet, "it is significant that historically and mythologically . . . Mandaeans consider themselves former Jews. In this context it is worth mentioning that the language of the Babylonian Talmud is quite close to the classical Mandaic."[38] It is also of interest that one of the Mandaeans interviewed for this book insisted, based on his research of his own lineage, that they were descendants of the Jewish people.

---

35. Buckley, *The Mandaeans*, 49.
36. Muhibbu-Din, "Ahl Al-Kitab and Religious Minorities in the Islamic State," 111.
37. de Blois, "The 'Sabians' in Pre-Islamic Arabia," 39–40.
38. Buckley, *The Mandaeans*, 4.

RELATIONSHIP TO JUDAISM

Many scholars contend that there is significant Jewish influence in Mandaeism. This is especially illustrated by the similarities of the priestly process that is discussed in detail in chapter 5. Both faiths prohibit eating meat from animals that have been killed by other animals, and require purification of the kitchens and tableware prior to their great holidays, *paruanaiia* for the Mandaeans, Passover for the Jews.

The Jewish holy book, the *Torah*, is considered false and full of lies by the Mandaeans, perhaps a view borrowed from the Muslims who consider it "corrupted." In fact, the sign of the Jews given to Abraham by God, circumcision, is considered abhorrent by the Mandaeans, to the point that if one is circumcised (even by an enemy), he is permanently excluded from the community. Yet, many of the practices of Mandaeans mirror Old Testament practices of the Jews, with the Mandaean priestly ordination following the Jewish priestly ordination very closely, as is shown in chapter 5. Table 2 provides a comparison of Judaism and Mandaeism.

Table 2. Mandaeism vis-à-vis Judaism

Comparison	Mandaean	Judaism (Old Testament)[i]
View of Old Testament	The Old Testament is "considered false and full of lies, an instrument of propaganda and oppression, invented by Yahweh and his followers."[ii]	Torah, the "teachings of the Five Books of Moses, is truth. A person must have faith in its essential, revealed character. A true Jew believes in revelation and the divine origin of the oral and written Torah."[iii]
Response to Circumcision	Prohibited; if circumcised, one is permanently excluded from community.	Required by God through the *Torah*, beginning with Abraham. (Gen 17:10–11)
Relationship of ethnicity & religion	Mandaean applies to both ethnicity and religious belief. However, if one abandons his religious belief, he is no longer considered part of the Mandaean ethnic group.[iv]	Jew applies to ethnicity and religious belief. However, to abandon religious belief does not separate one from the ethnic group.
Purification of tableware, kitchenware, pots, pans	In preparation for *paruanaiia*: by immersing all kitchenware in the flowing river water by priest, pronouncing over each item the name of Life and the name of *Manda d-Hiia*.	In preparation for Passover: by eliminating all leavening/yeast in the home.
Prohibition of eating meat	All approved animals must be killed and sacrificed by a priest or layman whose purity is intact before they are eaten. They cannot simply be killed and eaten.[v]	Animals killed by other animals are prohibited (Exod 22:31); "unclean" animals, those that did not have both split hooves and chewed cuds (Lev 11:2–3); and those of the sea that did not have both scales and fins. (Lev 11:9–12).

i. Old Testament comparisons are important as the Mandaeans believe they preceded the Jewish religion; however, one can see that many of their requirements seem to be developed in opposition to the Jewish beliefs of the Old Testament, which may not be followed by modern Jews of any sect.

ii. Lupieri, *The Mandaeans*, 36.

iii. Halverson, *Guide to World Religions*, 125.

iv. Lupieri, *The Mandaeans*, 5.

v. Ibid., 13.

RELATIONSHIP TO CHRISTIANITY

The Mandaeans have a strong aversion to Christianity even though their method of baptism by immersion initially appears to align them with Christianity. Thus, several scholars have gone to great lengths to dissociate these two religions by their baptismal practice, which is repetitive rather than initiatory. The Mandaean emphasis on baptism indicates a need for purification, cleansing of sin, and forgiveness, even though they deny original sin (for Mandaeans) and they have no standard definition of sin. Mandaeans contain a spark of the divine and bear responsibility for reconnecting with the Lightworld, based totally upon human effort through the repetitious baptisms.[39]

The relationship of Mandaeism to John the Baptist is murky. The veneration of John the Baptist and his parents, Elizabeth and Zechariah, is ironic as the Mandaeans deny he was the originator of baptism, or even the "baptizer par excellence."[40] In fact, they see his baptisms only as part of his priestly routines, but do credit him with being a great teacher. They seem to lack understanding of John's baptism as a sign of repentance, not as a method for salvation (Acts 19:4). The internal conflict within Mandaeism is illustrated by their adoration of John the Baptist, a circumcised Jew, and their abhorrence of the practice of circumcision.[41] Furthermore, all other characters in the Mandaean mythology existed as humans in their pre-celestial status. There are, however, no characters in the world of light that bear John's name, and no stories exist of his personal double. Neither does John appear in any apocalyptic texts, so in spite of being a figure of extraordinary standing, and although in some texts there is an attempt "to exalt him as a superhuman and semi-divine being, in the Mandaean religious consciousness he has always remained only a human being."[42] As part of their syncretistic pattern, however, Mandaeans accentuate small points of resemblance to people of other faiths. "To inquirers they will say, 'John is our prophet like Jesus' (or 'Muhammad', as the case may be) 'is yours.'"[43] The convenience of declaring the name of John to Christians, and to invoking

---

39. However, even as the Mandaean clergy dissociate their religion from Christianity, among the lay people, the Mandaeans speak of Christianity and Mandaeism as "cousins," possibly referring to the kinship between John the Baptist and Jesus.

40. Lupieri, *The Mandaeans*, 162–63.

41. Ibid., 111.

42. Ibid., 162.

43. Drower, *The Mandaeans of Iraq and Iran*, 2.

tolerance from Muslims, appears to be the primary importance of John, as opposed to any theological impact from him.

There is a strong Mandaean polemic against Jesus, calling him the greatest false prophet. References to Jesus, "for the most part refer to the practices of Byzantine Christianity which awake horror in Mandaeans, such as the use of 'cut-off' (i.e. not flowing) water for baptism, and the celibacy of monks and nuns."[44] Yet the Mandaean deities bear a resemblance, as *Anus* is the miracle worker similar to Jesus.[45] However, in true Gnostic form, the conflict between good and evil existed in Jesus, with some legends presenting Jesus as a negative demonic reality. Others portray him as a "direct emanation of the very heart of the divine" who took over a fleshly body to save them.[46] All Mandaean legends agree that Jesus never suffered the passion but rather escaped the earthly body and watched a substitute endure the cross (a view consistent with Islam). By this reversal of the event, they have been able to reconcile their own ideas of a messiah.

The baptismal ritual meal of water and bread is reminiscent of the Christian communion supper. The Mandaean holy day is Sunday, the same as Christianity, but for vastly different reasons. While Christians worship on Sunday to commemorate Jesus' resurrection, Mandaeans honor Sunday as the first day of the week as a tribute to the sun.

44. Ibid., 3.
45. Buckley, *The Mandaeans*, 8.
46. Lupieri, *The Mandaeans*, 37.

Their legends often contain elements of Christianity and/or Judaism, but with deviations and elaborations. The legends of Mary, for example go to extreme lengths to preserve her apart from her Jewish birth and her relationship as Jesus' mother.

Finally, there are a number of passages in Mandaean texts where the physical world is seen in a positive light and considered the direct creation of the highest, good divinity. "These passages must have been redacted in periods of clear cultural dependence on Christianity, or perhaps on Islam."[47]

RELATIONSHIP TO ROMAN CATHOLICISM

The Mandaeans' relationship to Roman Catholics dates to the sixteenth century when the Portuguese maintained a trading station in the current location of Basra, Iraq. Portuguese Catholic missionaries mistakenly identified the Mandaeans as "Christians of Saint John." Assuming the Mandaeans were simply unaware of the gospel of Christ, similar to the Ephesian disciples Apollos met who had received the baptism of John the Baptist but were unacquainted with the full gospel of Jesus (as recorded in Acts 18:26, 28; 19:5), the Catholics tried to convert them by force.

Several traditions of Mandaeism seem to have developed as a polemic against Catholicism. For example, Catholicism requires priests to be celibate, whereas Mandaeism requires priests to be married to at least one wife. "Several polemical Mandaean texts view with horror and disgust Christian monks and nuns who 'cut off life.'"[48] Probably the most striking similarity is the belief in purgatory, which may have originated during the period of Portuguese influence. Both the Catholic and Mandaean sects believe in a place of suffering to purify one before he goes to heaven/Lightworld. Both believe that the length of time in purgatory is dependent upon the type of sin, which determines the amount of purification required. Both pray for the dead at specific time intervals. However, Catholics pray for the judgment of the soul, "never taking for granted that the soul is sure of heaven."[49] In contrast, the Mandaeans pray for the souls to have strength for the next level of their journey to the Lightworld. True salvation occurs at death, which begins the soul's journey toward divinity, but its destination

---

47. Ibid., 38.
48. Buckley, "Libertines or Not," 25.
49. Smith, *The Teaching of the Catholic Church*, Vol. 2, 1171.

is not in question, only the time required to attain it.[50] Finally, the Mandaeans' acceptance of Mary's virginity, and the birth of Jesus through the mouth to preserve her virginity, has been viewed as an example of the Mandaean culture "for centuries impregnated with forms of deliberate religious equivocation aimed at attracting the sympathies of the successive Western people they came into contact with."[51] Table 3 summarizes the similarities and differences between Mandaeism and Catholicism.

The Mandaeans were exposed to a number of Catholic traditions based on the long occupation by the Portuguese, whose aim was to spread their Catholic religion. The Mandaeans were always anxious to include acceptable practices in order to avoid persecution by the Muslims by trying to appear like "People of the Book," whom Islam protected from persecution. Exposure to other traditions also served to create traditions of the Mandaeans to align or appeal to those of other religions.

---

50. Lupieri, *The Mandaeans*, 30.
51. Ibid., 121.

Table 3. Mandaeism vis-à-vis Roman Catholicism

Doctrine	Mandaeism	Roman Catholicism
Baptism	Repetitive baptisms, by immersion. Daily, for personal purification. Weekly, on Sundays, and during sacred holidays, in sequences of three, during solemn ceremonies led by the priests, who repeat specific prayers and adhere to specific rituals. There are several effects of the Mandaean baptism: 1. It reduces, but does not eliminate, the quality and quantity of punishment in the next world.[i] 2. Forgiveness of sins past and present, purification, blessing, and healing. 3. The most significant effect is allowing the soul a means of sharing in the Lightworld and of being in communion with ancestors who have already died and gone to that world.[ii] Feast days tend to be baptism days for Mandaeans who may otherwise neglect the ritual.[iii]	"An exterior washing of the body under a prescribed form of words."[iv] Candidates can be "plunged in flowing water" or a "still water of a pool" or, if there is not enough water for immersion, "then water may be poured three times on the head."[v] Immersion, pouring on head, or sprinkling all are acceptable, but the custom of immersion is always three times to signify three days of Christ's burial.[vi] Baptism is required for salvation, cleansing of sins, and admission to heaven; without baptism "it is impossible to go to heaven."[vii] Cannot be saved without baptism except in specific circumstances where baptism is not available. One becomes a part of body of Christ only through baptism.[viii] "Solemn administration of this sacrament (baptism) is reserved to the clergy." Though some specific exceptions can be made.[ix]
Baptism of Infants	Performed on newborns, including the giving of the child's astrological name, which is "calculated" by the priest.	Established by AD 160; for salvation until confirmation at the age of accountability. (7 years old).[x]
Role of Mary, Jesus's Mother	Mary is revered as the virgin mother of Jesus, who was a false prophet. According to their legend, she conceived by drinking spring water, as commanded by God. In order to preserve her virginity, she gave birth through her mouth.[xi] Mary became a Mandaean priest, *tarmida*, leaving the Jewish faith after the birth of her son, Jesus.	Mary is revered as the Mother of God; she lived with her sister after Joseph's death; she is free of original sin and actual sin; she is a perpetual virgin.[xii]

Doctrine	Mandaeism	Roman Catholicism
Marital Status of Priests	Marriage expected; polygamy practiced; expected that priests have children.	All religious clerics must be celibate, unmarried males. Celibacy has been written tradition since AD 385.[xiii]
Women as Religious Leaders	Historically there is evidence of women as *tarmida* (priests) and *ganzibra* (high priests).[xiv] Mary, the mother of Jesus was a *tarmida*. "The earliest attested, named historical person in Mandaeism is the woman Slama" from AD 200 who was a priest/scribe. There is also a woman priest, Haiuna, in the 7th Century.[xv]	All religious clerics must be celibate, unmarried males.
Role of Water	Water is considered sacred, but only if it is flowing, which then makes it "alive." It is used for purification through immersion baptism and ceremonial drinking. It cannot be used if in a pool, tub, or otherwise stagnant, non-flowing state. Mandaeans believe that running water draws its vital power from the heavenly river of light and life. This power is present in every course of water on earth in the ratio of one to nine; it is absent from non-flowing water.[xvi]	Necessary for salvation. Rite of washing with water signifies spiritual cleansing.[xvii]
Unforgivable Sin	For priests: adultery.[xviii]	No sins are unforgivable.[xix] Only one who has refused to seek pardon through Christ is unforgiven, as he will not ask for forgiveness.[xx]

History and Sources: Mandaeism

Holding Place for Dead Before Judgment	Mandaeans believe in a holding place that the souls pass through on their way to the Lightworld. It is a dangerous voyage because the heavens are inhabited by demons or evil beings who test the souls according to their impurity at the time of their death. Meals for the dead are held on the first, third, seventh, and 45th days after death ritual to give the souls strength to get to the next level. Souls that have not led pure lives according to Mandaean observance are imprisoned for various lengths of time along the way, for purification through suffering.[xxi]	Purgatory is a place of suffering for a time after death for un-repented/unforgiven sin or for sins "whose due punishment is to be completed after death."[xxii] "Through the purifying power of suffering, purgatory prepares souls for eternal life on their way to heaven.[xxiii] The sufferings in Purgatory are to free the soul to enter its heavenly reward.[xxiv] "These sufferings can be replaced by the intercessions of the church on earth for the soul."[xxv] The length of time in Purgatory is uncertain, depending on the type of sin and the state of the heart toward God at the time of death.[xxvi]
Relationship to the Dead	True salvation occurs at death, which allows the soul to rise and leave earth toward divinity.[xxvii] Ritual meals for the dead are held at weddings, anniversaries, ordination ceremonies, and holidays.[xxviii] "Every moment of the community's ritual life, all their forebears, from Adam to John the Baptist, through the great priests of the past and the closest relatives of those present, can and should be invited to the community meal."[xxix]	Praying for the dead begins at death, on the day of burial, and on the third, seventh, or 30th day after death, and on the anniversary of death. Additionally, daily Mass may be said. All Souls' Day—November 2, several holiday/masses throughout the year. "The dead must always be prayed for . . . but only for the Catholic," until the end of the world.[xxx] "The doctrine of Purgatory is not learned from Scripture . . . but these texts were written by men who, in the Jewish church or in the Catholic Church, already knew this doctrine."[xxxi] "Prayers for the dead refer not to Purgatory but to judgment," never taking for granted that the soul is sure of heaven.[xxxii]

i. Lupieri, *The Mandaeans*, 16.
ii. Buckley, *The Mandaeans*, 83; "Mandaean Baptism," 29.
iii. Buckley, *The Mandaeans*, 81.
iv. Smith, *The Teaching of the Catholic Church*, Vol. 2, 769. Some of these teachings appear contradictory and some have been changed since the publication of this book, but would have been in effect during the time the Mandaeans were being influenced by the Roman Catholic Church.
v. Ibid., 770.

vi. Ibid., 771–72.
vii. Ibid., 675.
viii. Ibid., 675–76.
ix. Ibid., 789.
x. Ibid., 794, 836.
xi. Lupieri, *The Mandaeans*, 120–21.
xii. Smith, *The Teaching of the Catholic Church*, Vol. 1, 515, 520–22, 527.
xiii. Smith, *The Teaching of the Catholic Church*, Vol. 2, 1061.
xiv. Lupieri, *The Mandaeans*, 13.
xv. Buckley, *The Mandaeans*, 4, 5.
xvi. Lupieri, *The Mandaeans*, 13–14.
xvii. Smith, *The Teaching of the Catholic Church*, Vol. 2, 767.
xviii. Lupieri, *The Mandaeans*, 16.
xix. Smith, *The Teaching of the Catholic Church*, Vol. 1, 608.
xx. Smith, *The Teaching of the Catholic Church*, Vol. 2, 962.
xxi. Lupieri, *The Mandaeans*, 31–32.
xxii. Smith, *The Teaching of the Catholic Church*, Vol, 2, 1141.
xxiii. Ibid., 1147–48.
xxiv. Ibid., 1155.
xxv. Ibid., 1155.
xxvi. Ibid., 1159.
xxvii. Lupieri, *The Mandaeans*, 30.
xxviii. Ibid., 32.
xxix. Ibid., 23.
xxx. Smith, *The Teaching of the Catholic Church*, 1162.
xxxi. Ibid., 1166.
xxxii. Ibid., 1171.

RELATIONSHIP TO ISLAM

A critical survival feature for Mandaeism has been its monotheism. Since the seventh century its adherents have lived under Islamic rule, and their continued existence has depended on being considered *ahl al-kitab* by Muslims. It remains a crucial survival strategy today. In 1980, the Mandaeans in Iran were stripped of their protected status by Ayatollah Khomeini. In 1995, he revised his opinion and issued a *fatwa*, a cleric's opinion "that the Mandaeans possess the requisite characteristics to be recognized as a 'people of the book.'"[52] As required by the Qur'an, Khomeini reiterated these requirements, "stating that they seemed to be monotheists with a holy scripture and a prophet and should therefore be recognized as a protected religion."[53]

In 2001, then-President Saddam Hussein of Iraq praised the Mandaean sect and pledged to build a temple in Baghdad for its followers. In this same address, he promised that the Mandaeans "would keep their equality with Muslims and Christians," the two main religions in Iraq."[54]

Similarities with Islam include fasting, giving alms, and prayer rituals. Mandaeans are required to pray three times a day, whereas Muslims are required to pray five times a day.[55] Praying facing a specific direction is also unique to each of these religions, with Muslims facing Mecca and Mandaeans facing the north, because they consider the North Star to be the throne of *Abatur*, who will in the end judge all mortals.[56]

Both religions contain elements of secrecy, as the lay people are neither capable nor permitted to read their holy books. Islam's requirement that its holy book, the Qur'an, only be read in Arabic results in eighty percent of the world's Muslims being unable to the read the Qur'an; thus, those who cannot read Arabic must rely on the *imams'* interpretations of their scriptures.[57] The Mandaeans limit their holy books to the clergy except in rare instances where laypersons are capable of reading the ancient Mandaic language.[58] Even in the 1930s, "few lay Mandaeans know their own script or

---

52. Buckley, *The Mandaeans*, 60.
53. Buckley, "With the Mandaeans," 8.
54. Reuters, "Saddam praises Sabaeans, pledges to build temple."
55. Drower, *The Mandaeans of Iraq and Iran*, 3. Legend attributes the diminution of prayer from five times to three times a day to John the Baptist.
56. Lupieri, *The Mandaeans*, 15.
57. Caner, *When Worldviews Collide*, 132.
58. Buckley, "Glimpses of a Life," 48; Lupieri, *The Mandaeans*, 10.

holy books; such studies are left to priests" whose number was diminishing even then.[59] Thus, the scriptures contained in the holy books of Islam and Mandaeism are not readily available to the laypeople.

Both the *imams* of the Muslims, and the *tarmidas* of the Mandaeans, are considered endowed with special knowledge and are seen in most cases as leaders of the local community of believers. Shiite Muslim clerics and Mandaean priests are both regarded as civil as well as religious leaders.[60]

Purification rituals are strong in both traditions. Muslims are required to perform the *wudu* (ablution or cleansing) prior to each prayer. Mandaeans are required to perform cleansing rituals in the form of immersion baptism, *masbuta*, at least weekly and more often if sin requires it. Mandaeans also practice *risama*, a daily cleansing process of all parts of the body and especially before participation in any religious ceremony. Additionally, the Mandaean practice of self-immersion is performed during the week in cases of contamination while awaiting the *masbuta* on Sunday.

Lamenting or grieving over the dead is prohibited in both traditions; however, the destiny of the dead is drastically different. Hell is an ever-present reality in Islam with no assurance of one's final destiny. The souls of Mandaeans are assumed to be destined for the Lightworld. It is simply a process to negotiate the ascent to the Lightworld. Muslims and Mandaeans both believe there are seven levels in the underworld. However, Mandaean literature devotes little attention to the underworld, while Islam specifies which categories of people will be in each level.[61]

Both Mandaeism and Islam revere Mary, the mother of Jesus, and believe she was a virgin. While Islam views Jesus as a prophet, Mandaeism rejects Jesus, saying he is a false prophet and both religions disavow his crucifixion.[62] Like Islam, Mandaeism believes Jesus was taken away while a substitute endured the cross.

Both faiths hold Adam in high esteem. Islam identifies Satan's sin as refusal to worship Adam. For the Mandaeans, Adam was the first to be instructed in the ritual and necessity of baptism and is thus the progenitor of this tradition.

While there are many similarities to Islam, it must be remembered that Mandaeans have lived under Muslim rule since the seventh century

---

59. Drower, *The Mandaeans of Iraq and Iran*, 51.
60. Lupieri, *The Mandaeans*, 10.
61. Caner, "Doctrines of Islam."
62. Caner and Caner, *More than a Prophet*, 62

and clearly have been influenced by their surroundings. This is particularly noteworthy as one considers the necessity of being labeled *ahl al-kitab*. Thus, it is not surprising that many elements of Islam appear to be mirrored in the Mandaean traditions. Table 4 summarizes the comparison of Mandaeism and Islam.

Table 4. Mandaeism vis-à-vis Islam

Comparison	Mandaeism	Islam
Main Elements	• Monotheism. • Baptism (at least weekly). • Prayer three times/day, facing north. • Fasting applies to anything that distorts man's relationship to God; abstinence from meat at certain times of the year. • Alms-giving (moral and material). • In addition to these main tenets, Mandaeans also stress the importance of marriage.	• Monotheism is expressed by *Shahada*, a declaration of belief that Allah is one and Muhammad is his prophet. • Prayer (*Salat*), five times/day, facing Mecca. • Fasting (*Sawm*), 30 days during Ramadan, during the sunlight hours. • Alms-giving (*Zakat*), 2.5 percent of wealth. • Pilgrimage, the *Hajj*, to Mecca if physically and financially able. • Also stressed, although considered optional by some sects, is the Muslim holy war, *jihad*. *Jihad* may be interpreted as internal (as a spiritual struggle) or external (defending Islam).[i]
Primary Occupation	Jewelers: goldsmiths and silversmiths.[ii]	Muslims forbidden to work with gold directly.
Missionary Effort	No one may convert; must be born into religion.	Everyone must convert or be damned; conversion sometimes accomplished by force.
Prayer Direction	Prayer is always to the North. Mandaeans consider the North Star to be the throne of *Abatur*, who is the divine judge of all mortals.[iii]	Prayer is toward Mecca, birthplace of prophet Muhammad and the location of the *Kaba*, the Sacred Mosque. (Qur'an 2:143–44; 149–150)
Adam/Sin	Adam did not sin, but ate the fruit he was destined to eat in order to gain knowledge. "His salvation does not derive from repentance but from the knowledge that the divinity has bestowed upon him. Also, baptism . . . serves to maintain or recover the purity lost through contact with the physical . . .	Adam is to be worshipped by the angels; Satan's (*Iblis*) sin was refusing to worship Adam (Qur'an 7:11; 17:61). Adam was the first created being, was considered a prophet of God, and did recognize his nakedness after he sinned against God in the garden. (Qur'an 95:4; 7:27) However, his sin was removal

History and Sources: Mandaeism

Adam/Sin (*continued*)	There is no trace of Adam sinning in Mandaean texts.[iv]	from Paradise, and his punishment was toil upon the earth (Qur'an 7:24; 90:4).[v] There was no residual effect of his sin on humans.
Religious Leaders	The priest is the highest religious and civil authority and recognized by Islamic authorities; also called "sheik" and "king."[vi]	The Imam is the spiritual leader of the local mosque.[vii]
Access of Sacred Text/ Doctrine to Laypersons	Secretive: Knowledge of religious texts and mysteries reserved for priests. ". . . religious knowledge has been the sole privilege of priests and their families."[viii] However, there are also those "who are not priests, but who know how to read and write the classical Mandaean language. . . . they have access to the sacred texts and the knowledge those texts convey."[ix]	The Qur'an is to be read only in Arabic. If unable to read Arabic, must rely on imams for instruction. Only 20 percent of Muslims worldwide are able to read the Arabic Qur'an.[x]
Purification Rituals	1. Baptism (*masbuta*), immersion by the priest; Mandaeans are baptized every Sunday and on most holidays. Baptism "reduces (although does not eliminate) the quantity and quality of punishment in the next world for sinful or irregular behavior, and restores those who have been very seriously contaminated to a state a ritual purity."[xi] 2. Daily ablution (cleansing) of all parts of the body and before participation in any religious ceremony. 3. Self-immersion, in cases of contamination (of a long list of sins) while awaiting the *masbuta* on Sunday.	Ablution or cleansing must occur before each prayer. It involves: 1. Washing the hands up to the wrist three times. 2. Rinsing the mouth three times. 3. Cleaning the nostrils by sniffing water three times. 4. Washing the face from forehead to chin and from ear to ear. 5. Washing the forearms up to the elbows three times. 6. Passing a wet hand over the whole of the head. 7. Washing the feet up to the ankles three times, first the right, then the left.[xii]

Comparison	Mandaeism	Islam
Hell	Mandaeans believe in hell, an underworld of darkness, in contrast to the Lightworld. There are seven levels to the underworld. It is not a reality for Mandaeans as all Mandaeans will enter the Lightworld at some point.[xiii] When Mandaeans become extinct on earth, it will cease to exist. "Souls of wicked Mandaeans go not to the underworld but upward to be purified in suitable toll stations until they are fit for further ascent."[xiv]	Hell is accepted as factual. It is a place of eternal torture, a bottomless pit.[xv] The abode of sinners (Qur'an 4:97). The abode of Satan (Qur'an 38:85; 7:18). The majority of hell's dwellers are women.[xvi] Two surahs teach that Christians will go to paradise (2:62; 5:69) and two surahs teach that Christians will go to hell (5:72; 3:85). Throughout Muslim thought, hell always seems much nearer than Paradise.[xvii] Every Muslim will spend some time in hell (surah 19:71) except those who die in *jihad*; they will go immediately to paradise. There are seven levels to hell, the shallowest reserved for those who believed in Allah but who ignored his commands. The deepest level is reserved for "religious hypocrites." The sixth level is for Christians and the fifth for Jews.[xviii]

i. Ankerberg and Weldon, *Facts on Islam*, 11–13.
ii. Lupieri, *The Mandaeans*, 6. To this day, jewelry making continues to be the primary occupation of Mandaeans, resulting in many kidnappings by Muslims, hoping to attain large ransoms. This information was given to this author in repeated visits with Mandaeans in the Middle East and in America.
   iii. Ibid., 15.
   iv. Ibid., 45.
v. These passages are an example of inconsistency in the Qur'an, where Adam is not only a sinner, but because he repented immediately, and did not place blame elsewhere, God forgave and elevated him.

vi. Lupieri, *The Mandaeans*, 10.
vii. Caner and Caner, *Unveiling Islam*, 249.
viii. Buckley, "Glimpses of a life," 48.
ix. Lupieri, *The Mandaeans*, 10.
x. Caner, *When Worldviews Collide*, 132.
xi. Lupieri, *The Mandaeans*, 16.
xii. Caner and Caner, *Unveiling Islam*, 123–24.
xiii. Buckley, *The Mandaeans*, 40.
xiv. Ibid., 8–9.
xv. Caner and Caner, *Unveiling Islam*, 122, 145, 148.
xvi. Ibid., 134.
xvii. Ibid., 33.
xviii. Caner, "Doctrines of Islam."

RELATIONSHIP TO THREE MAJOR WORLD RELIGIONS

In summarizing Mandaeism's syncretism with these three major world religions, it is somewhat difficult to clearly identify which has been the influenced, or the influencer, on several levels. While Mandaeism claims to be the world's original and oldest religion, citing Adam as its founder, historical evidence does not support that claim. Some scholars date Mandaeism to the third century CE, while others date it at the start of the Christian era in the first century.[63] Islam was clearly developed by Muhammad in the seventh century CE, and the earliest evidence for Mandaeism is the fourth century CE. However, as discussed earlier, Mandaeism, even though assumed to be older than Islam, is noted for accepting elements from others and reshaping them to fit the Mandaean belief system. It is also of interest that in the Mandaean system, all of the traditions or belief elements are initiated by God and copied from the Mandaeans by subsequent groups.

It is the view of this author that of the major world religions considered in this book, Judaism is the oldest, followed by Christianity. The Scriptures began with the Jews in the Old Testament and continued with the Christians in the New Testament. Christians consider that the Scriptures were completed in the first century AD. Islam followed, chronologically, by Muhammad's claim of hearing additional revelation from God through Allah's messenger, Gabriel. After Muhammad's death, his followers recorded his orally-transmitted words, creating the Qur'an. Islam then imposed the rule that any religion tolerated by Muslims must be able to produce a holy or divine book. This resulted in Mandaeans recording their oral legends in the *Ginza*, thus enabling them to become a protected, or at least a tolerated, religion by Muslims.

Sacred places were initiated by God, who claimed his holy mount, known as Mt. Moriah in Abraham's time, Mt. Zion in King David's reign, and Jerusalem in the New Testament era. Islam followed this model, by naming three holy places for its followers: Mecca, the birthplace of Muhammad; Medina, the final resting place of Muhammad; and Jerusalem, the location of Muhammad's translation into heaven. The Mandaeans have strayed from this model somewhat, by initially claiming the Jordan River as their holy site. They eventually expanded their definition of "holy" to include any flowing water, regardless of its location.

---

63. Reinke, "Mandaeans in Iraq," 9.

God initiated a holy day to be set aside for worship, the Sabbath of the Old Testament (Exod 16:23; 20:8). Most of Christianity claimed Sunday to honor the risen Jesus (John 20:1, 19, 26; Acts 20:7; I Cor 16:2). Islam also claimed a holy day, Friday, as the day of assembly (Qur'an 62:9). The Mandaeans designated Sunday as their holy day, in honor of the sun and the first day of the week. This is the time for baptisms and other religious activities, although secular business pursuits on Sunday are not prohibited.[64]

All three of these major religions are monotheistic, recognizing one God. However, the attributes and character of the Supreme Being of Islam and Mandaeism are quite different from the God of Judaism and Christianity. And while Judaism and Islam disavow a triune nature of God, Christianity and Mandaeism share a view of a triune God. In Mandaeism, however, the trinity is comprised of three celestial beings who do not include the Supreme Being.

The view of sin and salvation constitutes a significant difference between Christianity and other religions. The belief in sin and salvation basically drives all practices and rituals developed in each sect. While heaven and hell are a reality for all four of these (to a lesser degree for modern Jews), and a final day of judgment exists in each, the inhabitants of these final dwelling places and the paths to these eternal locations are very different. Of the four religions under consideration, only Christianity adheres to the belief of original sin through Adam to all humans.[65] Thus, for all branches of Judaism, Islam, and Mandaeism, sin is committed by breaking the rules of the religion involved. For Islam, it is rejecting "right guidance." For Judaism, sin is breaking the commandments of the Law, social action, and societal rather than individual. For Mandaeism, sin is wrong committed against others and some other specific acts. The basic way to salvation in Islam and Judaism is through good deeds, and in particular, more good deeds than bad deeds. For Mandaeism, forgiveness for sin comes through baptisms. Ultimately, in Mandaeism, all Mandaean souls will return to the heavenly Lightworld, so the only penalty for sin is the amount of time it takes to ascend to the Lightworld. If a person does not have enough baptisms to cover his wrongs, he will need to pay penalties along the way to the Lightworld after death. How severe or time-consuming the penalties are depends on the degree of wrongdoing and upon the prayers of those

---

64. Drower, *The Mandaeans of Iraq and Iran*, 96.

65. There are some sects of Christianity, both present and past, who do not hold this view of original sin.

still alive. For Christianity, forgiveness of sins has been achieved through the death and resurrection of Jesus Christ; and salvation is received by accepting or believing in that historical fact and receiving Jesus as one's savior. By accepting Jesus, one *has* eternal life (emphasis added) (John 3:16, 36; 11:25–26).

CONCLUSION

Given that many Mandaean beliefs have parallels in Christianity, there are many opportunities to build bridges of understanding between these two faiths. Knowledge and truth are very important to Mandaeans. While their belief that they possess the ultimate truth is a strong characteristic of their belief system, history has shown their ability to incorporate new truths into their belief system. The Bible teaches that those who seek truth will find it (Deut 4:29; I Chr 28:9; Matt 7:7). This chapter has described many doctrines of Christianity that have reflections in Mandaean doctrines. In fact, virtually every major element of Christianity has a counterpart in the syncretized beliefs of Mandaeism. This understanding of their world provides bridges of opportunity for sharing the gospel message of Jesus Christ, the only and ultimate truth man can know. Understanding Christianity's response to each of these comparative elements addresses issues faced by all truth-seekers, beginning with one's purpose on earth and concluding with one's eternal destination. A summary of these comparisons and contrasts is displayed in table 5.

Mandaeism claims to be the first world religion, yet many of its practices and traditions seem either adapted to, or in protest of, these three major world religions. Thus, it is significant to compare the general beliefs of each with Mandaeism.

History and Sources: Mandaeism

Table 5. Mandaeism vis-à-vis Three Major World Religions

Comparison	Mandaeism	Judaism	Christianity	Islam
Origin	There is no specific founder of Mandaeism. Adam was considered the first Mandaean. John the Baptist was the last messenger. First writings are from mid-seventh century.	Abraham (Gen 12) Some commentators assert that Judaism was formalized around 200 BC when rabbinic Judaism developed as distinct "from the religion of ancient (Old Testament) Israel."¹	Jesus, approximately AD 33.	Muhammad, AD 632, upon his death.
View of Prophets	Adam received the last fragment of light from the creator; he did not sin in the garden but reaffirmed the right that made him like God by eating the fruit of the tree of knowledge. If there was sin, it was that Adam allowed himself to be seduced by Eve. When Adam became aware of his true spiritual self, he was taught baptism by the Great Revealer, making Adam the first Mandaean. He refused to die and lived 1,000 years. Seth—received the spirit of Light; died in place of his father, Adam. Enoch, Noah, Shem Zechariah—John the Baptist's father John the Baptist—most highly venerated prophet.	All Old Testament prophets. Mandaeism claims to be the first world religion, yet many of its practices and traditions seem either adapted to, or in protest of, these three major world religions. Thus, it is significant to compare the general beliefs of each with Mandaeism.	All Old and New Testament prophets (Matt 4:17).	Many Old Testament prophets are considered legitimate, though their lives and actions are retold according to the perspective of Muhammad as he perceived the Scriptures to be corrupted by men. Jesus is the only New Testament figure to be considered a prophet by Islam, although his character is revised according to their belief system.

57

The Mandaeans—Baptizers of Iraq and Iran

Comparison	Mandaeism	Judaism	Christianity	Islam
View of Prophets (*continued*)	Prophets abhorred by Mandaeans.[ii] Abraham refused to die; he is detested by Mandaeans because of circumcision.[iii] Moses refused to die. Jesus didn't die but went directly to heaven with a surrogate dying on the cross. Muhammad.			
Holy Book	The Great Treasure, The *Ginza* is written in Mandaic, the language of the Mandaeans since their beginning. It is a compilation of writings, legends, prayers, and hymns and reached its final form in the mid-seventh century, in time to present it to the Muslim authorities.[iv]	Torah "Old Testament" is the written Law. It includes the Pentateuch, the first five books of Moses; the Prophets; and the Psalms, poetry and hymns. Talmud contains the interpretation and rules accompanying the Torah, as written by rabbis to assist in following God's laws. (Acts 24:14–15)[v]	Holy Bible, the only and inerrant Word of God, spoken through prophets and through Jesus by the Holy Spirit (Heb 1:1–3; 2 Tim 3:16).	Qur'an, contains the words of Allah transmitted by Gabriel to the prophet Muhammad. Hadith, a collection of sayings and examples of Muhammad. It is the second most important book in Islam after the Qur'an.[vi] Muslims believe the Qur'an supersedes and corrects errors in the Bible.[vii]

History and Sources: Mandaeism

Holy Places	Jordan River, originally believed to be sacred, suggesting the sect's origination in Palestine. Now all flowing water is generically called *yardna*, Arabic for "Jordan."[viii] Any river is appropriate to use as it is flowing water from the Lightworld and thus is holy.	Jerusalem, God's Holy Mount Zion. Israel, God's covenant land to the Jews.	Israel/Jerusalem, the place of the origin of Christianity and historically "God's people" of the Bible. However, Christians do not necessarily revere these sites (John 4:21–24).	Mecca, the birthplace of Muhammad; place of the most Holy Mosque, the *Kaba*. Muslims are required to make one pilgrimage to Mecca in their lifetime. Medina, the place of death of Muhammad. Jerusalem, the place of Muhammad's translation into heaven; Dome of the Rock, built in AD 691 to commemorate translation.[ix]
Weekly Holy Day	Sunday: In honor of the sun and the first day of the week; "baptisms and religious exercises are enjoined, but otherwise, Sunday is an auspicious day for business."[x] Baptisms for all practicing Mandaeans take place every Sunday; "the ceremony lasts several hours, occupying nearly the entire morning."[xi]	Saturday: The Sabbath (Exod 16:23; 20:8).	Sunday: The Lord's Day commemorates Jesus' resurrection on the first day of the week (John 20:1, 19, 26; Acts 20:7; I Cor 16:2). It is noted that some Christian sects do consider Saturday their holy day, the Sabbath of the Old Testament.	Friday: "The Day of Assembly" (Qur'an 62:9–10).

The Mandaeans—Baptizers of Iraq and Iran

Comparison	Mandaeism	Judaism	Christianity	Islam
Supreme Being	Monotheistic, with several names: Life, Great Life, First Life, Lord of Greatness, King of Light, Powerful. The Great Life is a personification of the creative and sustaining force of the universe, but the personification is slight and spoken always in the impersonal plural, it remains mystery and abstraction. The symbol of "the Great Life is 'living water', that is flowing water, or *yardna*.[xii] *Manda d-Hiia*—Knowledge of Life—occupies the preeminent position among the celestial beings. *Anus* performs miracles in the style of Jesus and destroys Jerusalem.[xiii] Mandaeans view Yahweh as "the ignorant and evil God, who created the world, is easily angered and anthropomorphic . . . and tried to smother . . . knowledge."[xiv]	Monotheistic, with several names: G-d, Yahweh, Jehovah.	Monotheistic, represented in the Trinity: God the Father, Jesus the Son, and the Holy Spirit.	Monotheistic, named Allah.
Jesus	A negative, demonic reality, a creature the demiurge (Yahweh) made for the purpose of trapping the heavenly messenger within it. He did not suffer the passion, nor was he ever actually killed."[xv]	A good teacher. However, his role as Messiah is rejected.	The Messiah, as prophesied in the Old Testament; Son of God (John 3:16); Savior of the world (Acts 2:14–36).	A good prophet; Muslims affirm the virgin birth but deny the passion, death and resurrection of Jesus, claiming that a substitute was crucified in His place.

History and Sources: Mandaeism

Sin	Since Adam did not sin, the notion of "original sin" doesn't exist for Mandaeans. However, wrongs against others, or in conflict with their teachings, are considered "sin." Mandaeans believe they are the only people who are born without sin, but that they do sin by action or inaction. Thus, baptism(s) are required for sins and moral faults, the number depending upon the sin.	All branches of Judaism (Orthodox, Conservative, and Reform) reject the notion of "original sin." Orthodox believe sin is "breaking the commandments of the Law"; Conservatives believe sin is "moral or social action"; Reform believe sin is societal, not individual.[xvi] Since the Temple was destroyed in 70 AD, Jews have believed "that good deeds could atone for bad deeds and that by pursuing good works coupled with genuine repentance, one could be forgiven."[xvii]	Every person is born in sin as a result of Adam's sin, and thus needs to be forgiven of the guilt and penalty that sin requires. Sin causes separation between man and God, but atonement through Jesus Christ restores a right relationship between an individual and God (Rom 3:23, 5:12, 6:23, 5:8, 10:9–13; John 3:16; Heb 9:11–28).	Sin is considered rejecting right guidance. It can be forgiven through repentance. No atonement is necessary.[xviii] Sin is never paid for: it is weighed on a balance scale. The goal is to please Allah more than one offends Allah.[xix]
Salvation	"Comes from physical death, which allows the soul to rise. At the end of one's earthly existence the search has come to an end; the time for questions is over, and the time for answers has finally arrived. The heavens are open, and the human message can cross them in a voyage toward divinity; *Abatur* is the judge of the dead."[xx]	"Salvation' is not considered to be a Jewish concept, inasmuch as Jewish people presume a standing with God." Orthodox and Conservative Jews believe in prayer,	Comes from recognition of man's sinfulness and a decision to accept Jesus Christ as Lord and Savior of one's life.	Comes from doing more good than bad deeds in this life. No certainty about one's final destination, as it is determined by Allah and man cannot know Allah's decision.[xxii]

The Mandaeans—Baptizers of Iraq and Iran

Comparison	Mandaeism	Judaism	Christianity	Islam
Salvation *(continued)*		repentance, and obedience to God's laws. Additionally the Conservatives include the necessity of maintaining a Jewish identity. Reform Jews believe salvation is attained through personal and social improvement.[xxi]	(Rom 3:23; 5:8; 5:12; 6:23; 10:9–13; John 3:16–17; 17:3, 8; Heb 9:11–28). Some branches of Christianity add baptism or other sacraments as requirements for salvation.	
Day of Judgment; Jesus' Return	*Abatur* is the judge of the dead. We are living in the fourth, shortest, and last of four ages of human history; the earth will be destroyed from the air. In some texts, Jesus will return at the end of time; in others, *Manda d-Hiia* will return.[xxiii]	The Messiah will come and reign over Jerusalem.	Jesus will return to judge and reign over all (John 14:1–3; Matt 16:27; Mark 13:26–27; Rev 1:7–8; 20:11–15).	Jesus did not die, but "will appear to all just before the final judgment" battle victoriously and "establish a thousand years of righteousness."[xxiv] The Day of Assembly "will be a day of mutual loss and gain . . . And those who believe in Allah and work righteousness he will reserve them from their ills, and he will admit them to gardens beneath which rivers flow, to dwell therein forever" (Qur'an 64:9).

i. Halverson, *The Compact Guide to World Religions*, 122.
ii. Lupieri, *The Mandaeans*, 116, 162. These four are called the "four prophets of falsehood", 164–165. Lupieri notes on page 164 how the Mandaeans "dealt with all well-known biblical figures, whether from the Old and New Testaments. The founders of hostile or enemy religions, Abraham, Moses, and Jesus are turned into demons. Their predecessors, from Adam to Shem in the Old Testament and John [the Baptist] and his parents in the New, are transformed into Mandaean figures. In this way Judaism and Christianity can be considered a deviation from a pre-existing Mandaean reality."
iii. Ibid., 47, 65.
iv. Buckley, *The Mandaeans*, 5, 10.
v. Caner, *When Worldviews Collide*, 110.
vi. Caner and Caner, *Unveiling Islam*, 249.
vii. Ibid., 87.
viii. Lupieri, *The Mandaeans*, 14.
ix. Caner and Caner, *Unveiling Islam*, 46, 71.
x. Drower, *The Mandaeans of Iraq and Iran*, 96.
xi. Lupieri, *The Mandaeans*, 15.
xii. Drower, *The Mandaeans of Iraq and Iran*, xxi.
xiii. Buckley, *The Mandaeans*, 8.
xiv. Lupieri, *The Mandaeans*, 36.
xv. Ibid., 37.
xvi. Halverson, *The Compact Guide to World Religions*, 125.
xvii. Hamilton, *Christianity and World Religions*, 100.
xviii. Halverson, *The Compact Guide to World Religions*, 107.
xix. Caner and Caner, *Unveiling Islam*, 150.
xx. Lupieri, *The Mandaeans*, 30.
xxi. Halverson, *The Compact Guide to World Religions*, 126.
xxii. Caner and Caner, *Unveiling Islam*, 31.
xxiii. Lupieri, *The Mandaeans*, 52.
xxiv. Caner and Caner, *Unveiling Islam*, 221.

4

Membership and Community

INTRODUCTION

Mandaeans "belong in clearly defined communities. Identity is chiefly communal in nature."[1] While some scholars focus on individualism, particularly in the context of the baptismal ritual, it is impossible to disconnect the individual from the Mandaean community. Even baptism is not an initiatory ritual of personal transformation, but a ritual that reinforces and maintains the communal nature of the sect.

Membership in the Mandaean community is attained only through birth. Maintenance of the community is achieved through elaborate rituals, specifically the baptismal and death rituals. Reinforcement of the community is accomplished through the blood lines of the priests and the continued involvement between the living and the dead through the Mandaean festivals and celebrations.

The priests play an essential role in keeping the community intact. None of the rituals can be performed without them, and the current Diaspora, combined with the declining number of priest-candidates, severely threatens the ongoing cohesion of Mandaeism's adherents. During the Diaspora, Mandaean priests from other countries

> are now helping Mandaean exile communities maintain their religious traditions. In addition, Mandaean texts are being translated and a Mandaean magazine is being published in the Netherlands, Britain, and Iraq. The Mandaeans are also using the internet and have their own dedicated websites where there are forums that

---

1. Buckley, *The Mandaeans*, 85–86.

they can use to keep in touch with one another and strengthen the bonds that keep their community together.²

Understanding how a sect develops and maintains its sense of community is crucial to understanding its mindset. The nature of community membership involves initiation, salvation, and eternal destiny. The conclusion to this discussion demonstrates how Mandaean beliefs combine to provide opportunities for Christians to participate with the Mandaeans in their quest for eternal truth.

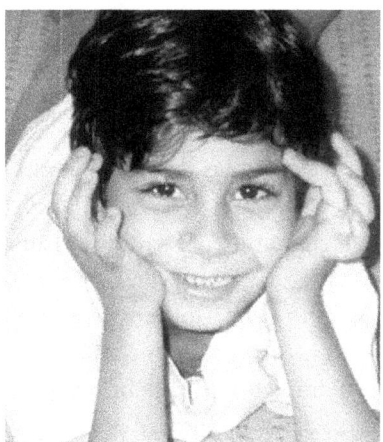

BIRTH RIGHTS

The Mandaeans are considered in a "state of arrested development" as their "cults, which are regarded by them as more sacred than their books . . . have been tenaciously retained [for centuries]; their ritual, in all its detail, most carefully preserved by a priesthood who regard a slip in procedure as a deadly sin."³ In spite of living among the Muslims for centuries, they have maintained their ancient traditions, including marriage only within their sect, and have continued their existence into modern times against extraordinary pressures. Though the Mandaeans "are only a handful of people, surrounded by neighbours [sic] of other faiths, they never mingle with

---

2. Reinke, "Mandaeans in Iraq," 8.
3. Drower, *The Mandaeans of Iraq and Iran*, xv.

them or admit them to intimacy; while a Subbi [Mandaean] who marries outside his race and creed automatically leaves it."[4]

Birth into the Mandaean community assures salvation. The Mandaeans believe they are the only people who have a link with the Supreme Being, having been endowed with a portion of his divinity at their birth. This conviction creates the exclusivistic perspective that is woven into their entire belief system. It makes them different from everyone else. In fact it not only elevates them "above everyone else . . . but also above God the creator and *his* laws."[5] This special endowment thus creates the boundaries of the sect and they are fiercely protected.

Marriage with outsiders is prohibited and conversions into the sect are forbidden. Though most scholars agree that the boundaries of membership in the sect are impenetrable, a recent publication concerned with the potential demise of the Mandaeans states that Mandaeism is not a proselytizing religion. There is no law prohibiting members of this faith community from converting to another religion or preventing members of other religions from converting to Mandaeism. However, marriage or forced marriage to someone of a different faith or forcible conversion results in a Mandaean losing their membership of [sic] the faith community.[6]

This statement contradicts volumes of research claiming conversion into the sect is not permissible, and indeed is a current example of the characteristically Mandaean flexibility to adapt to current circumstances.[7]

BAPTISM: PREPARATION FOR LIGHTWORLD

Baptisms are performed on newborns, at which time the priest announces the child's astrological name. The priest is responsible to calculate this name, providing several acceptable options to the parents who then select

---

4. Ibid., 1.

5. Lupieri, *The Mandaeans*, 35. The gnostic belief, though monotheistic, recognizes a lesser god as the creator, who is under the Supreme Being. As Mandaeans are endowed with the divinity of the greater God they are superior to the creator god.

6. Reinke, "Mandaeans in Iraq," 10.

7. Wisam, interviewed by author 16 Oct 2006. An interview with a Mandaean Christian, formerly a priest-candidate, points out that this is an example of "the new generation of priests bending the rules as the sect becomes smaller due to out-migration. To become Mandaean by the authority of some priests is to simply be baptized 366 times, the equivalent of the prior year of sin. However, circumcised men cannot convert, and all converts remain second class, never accepted as true Mandaeans."

the final name. This is the most important name of the four names Mandaeans have, and it is never revealed to strangers. This secret name is used only during religious rituals. "Unbaptized children are not considered to be a part of the faith community" until baptism.[8]

Routine baptisms generally begin at the traditional age of accountability, when a young person is considered able to distinguish between right and wrong. This is usually in the late adolescent or early teen years, between eleven and fourteen years of age. Once one begins the baptismal process, it is necessary to continue it throughout life. Repeated baptismal immersions "mark preparations and rehearsals for entry into that [Light] world, an entry that properly happens only at the death of the body."[9] Rather than being an initiatory ritual, baptism in Mandaeism is a "reaffirmation, consolidation with the Lightworld, and a reintegration with fellow Mandaeans past and present. . . . the [baptisms] re-create and reconfirm the . . . vital connection between the earthly world and the Lightworld."[10]

Baptisms are performed for everyone every Sunday. Additional baptisms for all occur at holiday festivals and at Mandaean funerals. Individuals may also baptize themselves between official baptismal occasions as the need arises (see chapter 6).

---

8. Reinke, "Mandaeans in Iraq," 10.
9. Buckley, *The Mandaeans*, 80.
10. Ibid., 83.

DEATH: ENTRY INTO THE LIGHTWORLD

"True salvation comes with physical death, which allows the soul to rise. At the end of one's earthly existence, the search has come to an end; the time for questions is over, and the time for answers has finally arrived."[11] One's eternal habitation is never in question, only the time it takes to ascend from the earth to the Lightworld. This time is spent going through a series of portals, called "toll" booths by Buckley and called "houses of punishment" by Lupieri. These portals are guarded by sentinels of the underworld and are a type of purgatory where the soul is examined and if necessary, penance is paid along the way. The penalty is dependent upon sins that have not been absolved through baptism. How quickly one ascends is also dependent upon the prayers of the remaining Mandaeans. All Mandaeans who have

---

11. Lupieri, *The Mandaeans*, 30.

passed on are always invited to the feasts and reunite in spirit with the living during their festivals. Thus, the connection between the living and the deceased is maintained in the community of believers.

Funeral rituals are an elaborate experience officiated by the *tarmida*. Other than the inability to properly practice baptism, the greatest difficulty facing dispersed Mandaeans is the inability to properly send their deceased into the Lightworld. "It is a difficult problem for Mandaeans in the U. S. exile who . . . without priests, cannot have proper death rituals."[12] They have been forced to rely on their own laypeople and clergy of other faiths to assist in these rituals. For Mandaeans to be without their own priests to carry out these rituals "is a very painful situation."[13] Mandaeans in America try to avoid the subject because the implications of dying without the priests and the proper flowing water are so immense. In fact, some Mandaeans have been known to return to Iraq to die, even in light of the desperate situation from which they escaped.[14]

CONCLUSION

Mandaeans live with the confidence that they are the chosen who will live eternally in the Lightworld, a heavenly "peaceful place of abundant food, music, fresh breezes, and no need to communicate by talking, for everybody knows what the others want."[15] However, one of the most painful conversations between scholar Buckley and members of the Mandaean community in America underscores the dependence of this paradise upon their rituals and, specifically, their priests to administer the rituals. While seeking asylum from the horrors of life under oppressive regimes, there is a strong desire to maintain their community in order to secure their eternal destination. This dependence upon the priests underscores the fragility of their system, which collapses when priests are not available to oversee the rituals that bind the community together.

Two major areas of opportunity exist for bridging understanding and discussing spiritual matters based on membership and community in Mandaeism compared with Christianity. First, the fragmentation and disintegration of their community provides the opportunity for discussion

12. Buckley, *The Mandaeans*, 29.
13. Ibid., 29.
14. Ibid., 29.
15. Ibid., 29.

of an eternity built on a better foundation, a foundation that is not dependent upon humans but which has already been provided by the sacrifice of Jesus and his completed high priestly activities on our behalf as presented in Hebrews 9:28 and 10:12. Secondly, the open invitation for all to come to Jesus is a sharp contrast to a system built on the odds of being born into the Mandaean community. This openness can be communicated through the life of Jesus and his encounters with those who were not born into the Hebrew faith, such as the Samaritan woman (John 4). The availability of salvation to all is further demonstrated in the encounter of Peter with Cornelius of Caesarea (Acts 10) and Paul's ministry dedicated to the Gentiles (Acts 9:15; Rom 11:13). The Bible states a clear invitation for all to come to Jesus regardless of ethnicity, birth, heritage, social status, or gender. Passages to reinforce this concept include: Gal 3:2–27; Col 3:11; John 3:16; 10:16, 28–30; Matt 28:19; and Rom 10:9–13.

5

Authority and Organization

INTRODUCTION

MANDAEISM CONSIDERS SEVERAL WELL-KNOWN biblical figures from both the Old Testament and the New Testament as founders of hostile or enemy religions. Those they do not like, such as Abraham, Moses, and Jesus, are turned into demons. "Their predecessors, from Adam to Shem in the Old Testament and John and his parents in the New, are transformed into Mandaean figures. In this way, Judaism and Christianity can be considered a deviation from the preexisting Mandaean reality."[1] Lupieri argues that this adaptation of biblical characters into Mandaean characters is clear evidence

> that Judaism and Christianity, with their Scriptures, already existed when Mandaeanism was formed. Further proof of this is supplied by the fact that the phenomenon does not repeat itself with . . . Islam, so that there is no seeking for anyone preceding the founder to turn into a Mandaean. . . . Islam [is] in fact considered a further degeneration of Judaism and Christianity, not directly a deviation from Mandaeanism. The fact that Judaism and Christianity, with their founders, receive such careful attention . . . proves that the specific variety of Gnostic syncretism that is Mandaeanism stems from Judaism and Christianity and splits off from them.[2]

The Mandaeans claim their beliefs and religion were formed by Adam. Their legends describe Adam being given a spark of the divine during his creation. He did not sin in the garden but reaffirmed the right that made

---

1. Lupieri, *The Mandaeans*, 164.
2. Ibid., 165.

him like God by eating the fruit of the tree of knowledge, actually fulfilling his destiny, gaining knowledge. That knowledge was given directly from *Manda d-Hiia* and included the methods and significance of baptism in order to reunite with the Lightworld. However, when it was time for Adam to die, legend says that he refused, and offered his sinless son, Seth, to die instead. This changed the order of things, having a child die before his parent. Thus, Seth, the obedient son, was the first human to enter the Lightworld. "Seth's purity above all other humans is ensured because he died instead of his father."[3] Other information claims there is no specific founder of Mandaeism, but that Abraham was considered a Mandaean (until he was circumcised) and John the Baptist was the last messenger and most recognized Mandaean prophet. However, "Shem [was] chosen by Mandaeans as their own founding father."[4] As the Mandaeans have traced the origins of various groups, one fact remains consistent in their mythology: they "are the only ones who are pure and genetically without sin."[5]

THE PRIESTLY ROLE

The Mandaeans make a clear distinction between priests and laypeople. Their society is stratified: priests (*tarmidas* and *ganzibras*), learned laymen (*yalufas*), and laypeople. Priests are expected to be married and have

3. Buckley, *The Mandaeans*, 36.
4. Lupieri, *The Mandaeans*, 51.
5. Ibid., 52.

Authority and Organization

offspring.⁶ This "high regard for marriage among the Mandaeans differs strikingly from the antipathy toward marriage held by the early Gnostics."⁷ Priests function as the head of the community in both a spiritual and civic sense. The *tarmidas* are of the lower priestly rank, and the *ganzibras*, are from the highest rank. The *ganzibra*, or high priest, also serves as the treasurer and is responsible for the preservation of the treasure of knowledge, the sacred book, the *Ginza*. The priests are "aristocratic . . . [and] enjoy enormous respect as ritual specialists and spiritual leaders of the people. Without them, traditional Mandaean society would not exist."⁸

There are many factors that are diminishing the ranks and practices of the Mandaeans in the current Diaspora, but probably the most significant is the declining number and distribution of priests throughout the world. The sect nearly became extinct in the 1830s when two cholera epidemics "erased the entire Mandaean priesthood, leaving a decimated and demoralized lay population. . . . [W]ithout priests to baptize, celebrate marriages, officiate at religious festivals and at ceremonies for the dead, the Mandaean religion could not—and still cannot—be sustained."⁹ Fortunately for the sect, two young men, sons of priests, initiated one another into the priesthood in a highly unorthodox manner, and in doing so, have preserved the sect for nearly 200 years to the present time.

Today, there are very few learned laypersons and very few young novices. The priestly responsibilities are carried on within the priestly families, but more of today's young men are choosing other occupations. While Mandaeans cite more leisure opportunities and more varied career choices, the status of Mandaean priests within their own community has changed considerably. No longer held in the highest esteem, priests are criticized for failing to communicate properly with adherents, "so that knowledge of their own written language and Mandaean religion is very limited. . . . Unless something is done soon to support the more spiritually inclined members of the younger generation and reinforce their knowledge of their religion in their country of origin and in the Diaspora, the pessimistic view that Mandaeism is on the verge of extinction will prove to be fully justified."¹⁰

---

6. Buckley, *The Mandaeans*, 98; Lupieri, *The Mandaeans*, 29.
7. Yamauchi, review of *The Mandaeans*, by J. J. Buckley, 136–37.
8. Buckley, "With the Mandaeans," 8.
9. Buckley, "Glimpses of a Life," 34.
10. Reinke, "Mandaeans in Iraq," 11–12.

THE PRIESTLY ORDINATION

The ordination process is very lengthy and follows to some degree the ordination of Levitical priests set forth in the Old Testament. There is a very precise and rigorous selection process for priest-candidates. In addition to the purity of the priest himself, the wives of all participants, the candidate, the teachers, and any other priestly assistants must be pure throughout the initial nine-day and eight-night period. If any of the wives are menstruating, about to give birth, or have a miscarriage during the ceremony, it would be invalid and all (male and female) would have to repeat the extensive purification rituals. Once the proper week is chosen, various baptismal and sacrificial rituals are carried out. A special ordination hut is constructed with the doorway facing north. The candidate is clothed in a new *rasta*, a garment also used in baptism, representing the candidate's death to the material world. He must then demonstrate to his teacher and all participants that "he possesses the necessary knowledge and preparation. He will recite from memory an entire sacred book, prayers, and the ritual for the dead."[11] The officiating priests follow along in the sacred book to assure that the candidate recites accurately, with no errors, while others prepare the sacred food. The candidate and his teacher must stay awake the entire week. "Just as the high priest of Jerusalem was kept awake the night before Yom Kippur, the Mandaean candidate to priesthood must not sleep. Both cases respond to the same fear: a nocturnal ejaculation could make the man who must approach divine things impure."[12] During the week, the priest-candidate remains in the hut to "pray, recite sacred texts, discuss things with his teacher and receive secret instruction."[13] If a candidate does become impure during this period, the ordination could be postponed for up to a year and a series of baptisms would be necessary.

When a priest-candidate completes this initial period successfully, he then begins a sixty-day period of isolation and purification. This involves separation from his wife and family, daily purification immersions, and preparation of his own food by special processes. At the end of the sixty days, the final initiatory act requires that the candidate recite the entire *masiqta*, the death mass, and perform the ceremonial actions that accompany this ritual. Only at the end is the candidate considered a true *tarmida*.

---

11. Lupieri, *The Mandaeans*, 26.
12. Ibid., 27.
13. Ibid., 27.

For a *tarmida* to advance to the *ganzibra*, he must participate in a special ceremony of one who is near death and who has lived a blameless life. This person, upon death, will be the messenger to the Lightworld, informing them of the new *ganzibra*.

RELATIONSHIP OF MANDAEAN PRIESTS TO ANCIENT JEWISH PRIESTS

Many scholars contend that there is significant Jewish influence in Mandaeism and this is especially illustrated by the similarities of the priestly ordination process. Priests in both Judaism and Mandaeism must be born into the priestly lineage, may never shave their heads or beards, and must be mentally and physically fit. The Mandaean priestly candidates are inspected for physical perfection prior to ordination. Levitical priests were prohibited from serving if a single imperfection was present (Lev 21:5). The rituals to ordain priests follow similar procedures, beginning with the cleansing of the body and the wearing of specific clothing. The ritual for the Mandaean *tarmida*, however, is far more extensive than that of the Levitical priest, lasting sixty-eight days, while the Levitical ordination lasted eight days. The Mandaean priest is required to memorize prayers and receives secret knowledge from the head priest during the sixty-day isolation period. Table 6 provides a summary of the ordination rites of the Mandaean priests compared with the ancient Jewish priests.

Table 6. Mandaean Priests vis-à-vis Jewish Priests

Comparison	Mandaean Priests	Jewish Priests (Old Testament)[i]
Requirements	Though priests may come from outside the "priestly class," most priests have a lineage of priests in the family. "A lay Subbi who has a 'clean' family history for the necessary number of generations and has the requisite physical and mental qualifications, can become a priest, but, in practice, the priesthood tends to run from father to son."[ii] "A certain family right usually holds true . . . the sons of priests usually become priests, especially as they move up in the hierarchical order."[iii]	Must be born into a priestly family, the Levites, descendents of Aaron, the first High Priest (Exod 29:10; 40:15; Num 3:10).
Hair	Priest/candidate may not cut hair beginning at puberty.[iv] Hair on the head is sacred, a mark of honor. Even laymen consider cutting the hair of the head or beard as impious.[v] (This requirement seems to have some connection to the biblical Samson, told as a folk tale in Iraq.)[vi]	Priests must never shave their heads or trim the edges of their beards (Lev 21:5).
Physical Perfection	"Must be perfect of body and mentally fit."[vii]	Priests may not have physical defects (Lev 21:16–23).
Importance of the Color Blue	Blue fabric not allowed, as it "symbolized the material aspect of this world."[viii]	High Priest's robe required to be entirely of blue cloth (Exod 28:31).

AUTHORITY AND ORGANIZATION

Ordination Ceremony	A ritual that takes a total of 68 days to complete: nine days and eight nights, plus a waiting period of 60 days until the priest-candidate is eligible to conduct priestly duties. 1. Preparatory ritual: double baptism, ram sacrificed, and verification of physical perfection of priest-candidate. 2. Candidate provided with special, specific clothing. 3. Candidate recites from memory an entire sacred book, prayers, and the ritual for the dead. 4. Candidate receives symbols of priesthood: crown, gold ring, ceremonial stick of olive wood. 5. Candidate receives secret instructions from mentor. 6. Priest cannot sleep for the entire nine-day/eight-night ceremony, for "fear of nocturnal ejaculation, which would make him impure" and result in postponement of the consecration ceremony for at least one year and/or a series from nine to 366 baptisms.[ix] 7. Priest is baptized in a series of solemn baptisms. 8. Priest is isolated and purified for 60 days. 9. Priest leads celebration ceremony for the dead for 60 days. 10. Priest offers sacrifice, prepares ceremonial bread and wine surrogate.[x]	A ritual that took eight days to complete. 1. Priest cleansed with water (Lev 8:6). 2. Priest provided special, specific clothing (Lev 8:7–9; 13). 3. Priest anointed with oil (Lev 8:12). 4. Ram sacrificed (Lev 8:22–24). 5. Unleavened bread (Lev 8:26). 6. Priest sprinkled with blood and anointed with oil (Lev 8:30). 7. Priest remained in Tent of Meeting seven days to complete the ordination (Lev 8:33–36).

i. Old Testament comparisons are important as the Mandaeans believe they preceded the Jewish religion; however, one can see that many of their requirements seem to be developed in opposition to the Jewish beliefs of the Old Testament, which may not be followed by modern Jews of any sect.
ii. Drower, *The Mandaeans of Iraq and Iran*, 146.
iii. Lupieri, *The Mandaeans*, 13.
iv. Drower, *The Mandaeans of Iraq and Iran*, 146.
v. Ibid., 166.
vi. Ibid., 165.
vii. Buckley, *The Mandaeans*, 98, 183 n.5.
viii. Lupieri, *The Mandaeans*, 26.
ix. Lupieri, *The Mandaeans*, 27. This same requirement was placed on the High Priest of Jerusalem on the night before Yom Kippur for the same reason.
x. Ibid., 25–29.

CONCLUSION

The responsibility of maintaining a tight community that is protected from outsiders is vested in the priests, who maintain a relationship between the material, physical world and the divine, spiritual world. From requiring priests to come from priestly families, to the lengthy ordination process, the priests are prepared and equipped to provide spiritual and civic leadership to the Mandaeans. Their repeated rituals are reminiscent of the repetitive rituals of the Levitical priests of ancient Judaism. However, the need for these repetitious rituals in Judaism was eliminated by Jesus, the ultimate high priest, who provided the final and purest sacrifice for all times for all people.

For Mandaeans who are particularly familiar with the priestly process, the opportunity exists for discussion regarding the priests of the Bible as compared with the priestly role and responsibilities in Mandaeism. The book of Hebrews in the New Testament presents an excellent study of this topic beginning with the qualifications of the high priest and ending with the rationale for the elimination of earthly priests as this role has been completed in Jesus, as outlined in chapters five through seven.

These passages provide the foundation for a discussion of the priestly responsibilities in Judaism in light of the new covenant in Christ, and could be the basis for discussion with Mandaeans about their priestly system, particularly the repetitious rituals. However, this topic represents only one aspect of apologetic discussion that is possible with Mandaeans and should, of course, be preceded by a solid foundation of friendship and trust.

6

Rituals and Holidays

INTRODUCTION

RITUALS REQUIRE EFFORT, DISCIPLINE, and belief that the effort is producing something of value to the participant. For Mandaeans, the work involved in the rituals makes the Lightworld accessible to the earthly inhabitants, binding living Mandaeans with their ancestors who have gone on before. Mandaean rituals are very specific, with complicated and precise requirements in words and deeds. When followed explicitly, which is the responsibility of the priest-administrator, there is no question in the minds of the adherents that the ritual is producing the desired link between the Lightworld and the human world. The purpose of this section is not to detail the intricacies of the ritual practice, but to provide an overview that presents the beliefs and outcomes the adherents expect to accomplish by the practice.

BAPTISM

The most obvious and well-known ritual of the Mandaean religion is their frequent use of immersion baptism (*masbuta*) for purification. Baptisms must take place in a river, in water that is flowing, living water (*yardna*). Yardna originally meant the Jordan River, but today applies to any flowing water. This water serves as the source of life and as a connection between the Lightworld and the earthly world, uniting Mandaeans with their ancestors who have gone on before them. Since the river water is not totally pure,

the baptism is preceded by the priest "binding the forces of darkness," and preparing the river for baptism.¹

In the current Diaspora situation, it must be noted that exceptions are being made for the requirement of baptism in flowing water. As it has become harder for Mandaeans to maintain their rituals according to tradition, those "traditions have decayed and ritual practices have been

1. Buckley, "Why Once is Not Enough," 28–29.

abandoned in modern industrial society."[2] Reports from countries outside the Middle East indicate that showers in private homes, swimming pools, and fountains are being used.

This connection between the Lightworld and earth through water comes from the Mandaeans' sacred book, the *Right Ginza,* XV 354, 12–13: "Thus the water gushed forth and the connection of this world was established. The sending of heavenly living water into the waters of the earth and the close association of the concepts of life, light, and water are the most important aspects regarding salvation in the Mandaean mythology."[3]

The chief characteristic of the Mandaean *masbuta* is its repeated enactment, contrary to the usual understanding of baptism as a singular, initiatory rite.[4]

> This constantly recreated redemption is, of course, balanced with the goal of final liberation from the earthly realm. Life on earth is neither free nor automatic, but must be continuously reconfirmed in its dependence on the Lightworld. Therefore, human responsibility for ritual action weighs heavily.... The continually repeated baptism serves to confirm and consolidate the Mandaeans in their two-world membership. Mandaeans make their Lightworld visible, tangible, and accessible through ritual work.[5]

This stems from their belief that baptism furnishes the only possibility for taking part in the Lightworld, and it affects their reintegration with fellow Mandaeans past and present. It recreates and reconfirms the connection between the two worlds: the world of the earthly Mandaeans and the world of their ancestors on high. Thus, the steady repetition of baptism is necessary. To abolish the repetitions would imply severance from the Lightworld and spiritual death.

Newborns are baptized within forty days of birth. At that initial baptism the infant is given his secret, astrological name. Baptisms of newborns generally occur in the spring or summer, unless the infant's life is in danger. Children are not generally baptized again until an age determined by the parents, generally at eleven or twelve years of age.[6] Baptisms are held every

2. Reinke, "Mandaeans in Iraq," 11.
3. Franzmann, "Living Water Mediating Element in Mandaean Myth and Ritual," 158.
4. Buckley, "Mandaean Baptism," 25.
5. Ibid., 32, 33.
6. Wisam, interviewed by author 16 Oct 2006. Because of the rapid out-migration of Mandaeans from the sect, there has been discussion of requiring child baptisms in order

Sunday and during every Mandaean holiday, but also after any personal defilement, especially after menstruation and following sexual intercourse. In order to maintain purity between priest-administered baptisms on Sundays or holidays, individuals may practice self-immersion between the official baptismal events.

Individuals being baptized wear a special white garment, a *rasta*. This same garment is worn by the deceased, "so one enters the water and the Lightworld [at death] in the same kind of garment."[7] The water is considered the "garment of light" for the baptized, rather than the material fabric being the garment of light.[8] During the baptism, "one has the impression that the barriers separating the world of light and the earth have disintegrated, that there is no longer a certain heaven and earth but a merging of the two in the experience of the ritual."[9] The priests are the mediators who cross between the boundaries of earth and the Lightworld on this heavenly journey, essentially participating in both worlds. "Mandaeans believe that life stops for a brief moment before starting again fresh and new after the baptism."[10]

to more directly tie young people to the sect. However, the official rules of the religion do not require child baptisms since the sins of children are considered insignificant.

7. Buckley, "Mandaean Baptism," 30.
8. Ibid., 29.
9. Franzmann, "Living Water Mediating Element in Mandaean Myth and Ritual," 160.
10. Reinke, "Mandaeans in Iraq," 10.

Rituals and Holidays

The procedure for baptism begins with the individual immersing himself three times. The individual is then immersed three times by a priest, followed by drinking river water from the priest's hand three times and engaging in a sacred handshake, signifying the giving of truth. The priest, with his wet finger, draws three lines across the individual's forehead, from left to right ear. The purpose of this action is unclear in the literature. Lupieri suggests this action possibly symbolizes the Christian sign of the cross, while Segelberg maintains that its meaning is unclear, but speculates that perhaps is a dedication to Hibil, Sitil, and Anus, the trinity of *utras* who are invoked in Mandaean prayers.[11] He then crowns the individual with a myrtle wreath, all the while reciting the potent names of Lightworld beings to protect the baptized person. After all have been baptized, the ritual continues on the river bank with each participant receiving a piece of special bread prepared in advance by the priest, drinking three servings of river water, exchanging the sacred handshake once again and throwing the wreath into the water. Throughout the ritual, the priest recites specific prayers for each aspect of the proceedings.

---

11. Lupieri, *The Mandaeans*, 16; Segelberg, *Masbuta*, 54.

The Mandaeans—Baptizers of Iraq and Iran

Among the "sealing" prayers offered by the priest is one that "asks for forgiveness of sins for past and present Mandaeans."[12] There are several effects of the Mandaean baptism, including forgiveness, purification, blessing, and healing. However, the most significant effect of baptism is providing a means for the soul to share in the Lightworld and to be in communion with ancestors who have already died and gone to that world.

John the Baptist is considered by recent Mandaean traditions as the only true prophet. It has also been noted earlier that there is an element of convenience in having had a prophet, in that it facilitated attaining *ahl al-kitab* protection by the Muslims. However, John the Baptist is not regarded as the originator or even the most important prophet in the Mandaean faith. "In the more ancient literary contexts, he does not act as a prophet, nor is he called one, except in an anti-Islamic function. The only prophecy that is recorded for him concerns the coming of Muhammad. . . . for the Mandaeans, John is not the Baptist par excellence (indeed, he is not even called "baptist," except in just one of the many passages that speak of him) since he was not the one who invented baptism. This was revealed to Adam by *Manda d-Hiia*, and so Adam is the initiator of the Mandaean ritual baptism on earth, and John learned it as a child from Anus."[13]

In the early twentieth century, German scholar H. Lietzmann "denied that the Mandaeans had anything to do with the disciples of John the Baptist and stated that the traditions about John in the Mandaean literature were derived from the New Testament and Christian legends via Syrian Christians and that they were introduced in the Mandaean texts as late as in Arabic times."[14] He further asserted that the baptismal rituals of the Mandaeans were copied from the Nestorians. Though Lietzmann's theories were eventually dismissed by other scholars, Segelberg predicted the imminent demise of the last of the gnostic sects and decried the fact that "it is still not possible to describe accurately and completely the central act of the Mandaean religion."[15]

WEDDINGS

Weddings are also an occasion for baptisms. They occur on Sundays and last one to two days. The wedding is, of course, officiated by the *ganzibra*,

12. Buckley, "Mandaean Baptism," 32.
13. Lupieri, *The Mandaeans*, 162–63.
14. Segelberg, *Masbuta*, 15.
15. Ibid., 18.

the high priest, without whom it would be invalid. The baptism of the bride is preceded by her silence until the purification process is complete. The bride is taken to the *mandi*, the cultic hut used for certain rituals, where she is examined to determine her virginity.

A special wedding hut is prepared in the groom's courtyard, which has no walls but decorations of flowers and various grasses and reeds. It is covered with a white veil, similar to a mosquito net. The actual wedding ceremony takes place in this wedding hut with the groom, the *ganzibra*, and a man representing the bride. The bride is not present and this representative answers all questions for her, officially accepting the groom on her behalf. The ceremony lasts for several hours, beginning with a ritual meal for the dead. The Mandaeans believe that all ancestors from Adam to John the Baptist to all of their forebears should be invited to all community meals, which include ritualistic foods and beverages. The foods are much richer in the wedding ceremony, but the sacredness of the food requires that it cannot be thrown away, nor used on other occasions. It must be distributed among the poor or discarded into the river.

Throughout the ceremony, the bride remains in the future home where she and her groom will live. Near the end of the event, one of the priest's helpers brings her two rings from the groom and in the presence of witnesses she is asked if she wants to marry the groom. After the final pronouncement of their wedded status, the participants throw rose petals, powdered sugar, and almonds over those present. Following the declaration of marriage, the marriage is consummated, based upon a time determined by the priest to be the most propitious time, usually within six hours of the ceremony.

FUNERALS

The Mandaean funeral ritual is complicated and significant to the final destiny of the soul. The death mass, *masiqta*, takes about twelve hours. However, the annual *masiqta*, occurring during the five-day holiday of *Paruanaiia*, requires even more time. Though several priests may be involved in the *masiqta*, at least one must be the *ganzibra*. The near-death of a blameless person (either a man or woman from a spotless priestly family or a married person with children) also provides the final step in the ordination process for a new high priest.[16] The deceased is given the responsibility to carry the message, the announcement to the Lightworld of a new *ganzibra*.

16. Lupieri, *The Mandaeans*, 29.

The funeral ceremony commemorates all deceased Mandaeans, inviting them to be present in the community. Simply pronouncing the names of the deceased "creates their presence . . . [and is similar to the way] that the word 'remembrance' should be understood in connection with the commemoration" of the Eucharist.[17] This is comparable to the celebration of the Eucharist in the Catholic Church, which represents the actual body of Christ present among the worshipers.

The funeral ritual varies slightly with the occasion, whether performed as part of the *Paruanaiia*, the ordination of the priest, or simply as a death mass. It always includes the sacrifice of a dove and special bread prepared by the priests. The ceremony cannot begin less than three hours after death. Loud wails and weeping are forbidden among the Mandaeans.

HOLIDAYS

The Mandaeans celebrate four major holidays, all of which include baptisms. "The feast days tend to become occasions for baptism for many Mandaeans who may neglect it at other times."[18]

The Great Feast, *Dihwa Raba*, is a two-day celebration of the New Year and Creation, which was completed on this day. During this time, all the spirits of light leave the earth, taking twelve hours to travel to the Lord of Greatness and pay their compliments. The powers of evil and death are left unrestrained on earth, so the community must remain in their homes for thirty-six hours. If someone dies during this time, the funeral is delayed until the festival's end. This holiday is also marked by the priest making predictions for the coming year.

The Feast of Golden Baptism, *Dihwa id Dimana*, celebrates the baptism of Adam. This one-day feast includes baptisms of all Mandaeans, including infants and children. If a person is baptized in a new *rasta*, the white baptismal garment, the baptism is the equivalent of sixty baptisms.

The Short Feast, *Dihwa Hnina*, also called the Little New Year, is a one-day feast celebrating the "return of *Hibil Ziwa* from the underworlds to the worlds of light."[19] It is a night of power, when, if a man is pious, he can obtain whatever he asks. If he is truly pious, he doesn't ask for worldly favors, but

---

17. Ibid., 32–33.
18. Buckley, *The Mandaeans*, 81.
19. Drower, *The Mandaeans of Iraq and Iran*, 88. *Hibil Ziwa* is a light spirit, the divine being most directly in touch with the earthly world.

freedom from sin and the blessing of spiritual gifts. If granted, the individual is informed through a vision. During this holiday, food is distributed to the poor, baptisms occur, and ritual meals are eaten honoring the dead.

The greatest holiday is the *Paruanaiia*, meaning "five."[20] This five-day, intercalary festival is a great celebratory feast held at the river. It usually falls in the early part of April when the rivers are swollen. This religious festival, with a great baptismal river feast, is a time to invite the dead to the sacred meal. It is considered an especially fortunate time to die, as the heavens are open and souls who die during this period go into the Lightworld without interference from the forces of evil along the way. Special preparations are made for the feast, including consecration of the *mandi*, the cultic hut used in the ordination of priests, and purification of the tableware and kitchenware of all members of the community. The members of the community who have died are invited to celebrate in the feasting of *Paruanaiia*.

20. The Mandaeans use a 365-day solar year, but do not have leap years. Thus, they have twelve months of thirty days, and between their eighth and ninth months, they add five days (intercalary), which are used for this feast.

RITUALS AND HOLIDAYS

CONCLUSION

While birth into the Mandaean sect gives special status in the universe, and the secret knowledge given only to Mandaeans is the key to salvation, the cultic rituals are the actions that achieve salvation as the soul departs the earthly world of darkness and soars to the soul's native world of light. The baptism ritual confirms and reconfirms the individual's salvation. "Still, the constantly created redemption remains incomplete, for it must be balanced at the end of the earthly life with the final liberation from this life."[21] It is thus the responsibility of the Mandaean to continue the baptisms throughout his/her lifetime, a heavy responsibility for any human to attain his own salvation.

21. Buckley, *The Mandaeans*, 85.

7

Signs and Symbols

LEGENDS AND VISIONS

THE MANDAEANS, LIKE MOST Middle Eastern people, have a strong sense of the supernatural. Their belief in an entire system of *utras*, messengers between earth and the Lightworld, is a clear example of this. Each *utra* has a specific purpose and most have reached this status after an exemplary life as a human. As noted earlier, John the Baptist is an example that this elevation to an *utra* is not always the reward for a prophet.[1]

Of particular note is the symbolism encompassing the celebration of *Paruanaiia*, the five-day intercalary holiday, which is steeped in superstition. This is regarded as a particularly favorable time to die since the souls of the dead do not have to go through the journey to the Lightworld with dangerous encounters. The gates of the Lightworld are open during these five days and souls enter directly. However, the five days preceding the *Paruanaiia* are a particularly inauspicious time to die, as the forces of evil are unusually rampant during those days.

Belief in the authenticity of visions is common among Middle Eastern peoples. The most visible and influential are the visions of Muhammad, which resulted in the Islamic religion. Individuals are often blessed or cursed by visions. The Mandaeans particularly look forward to visions to answer their desires during the *Paruanaiia*. This is the one time when a person can ask for anything, and if it is to be granted, this is communicated through a vision.

---

1. See chapter 3 for a discussion on the elevation of humans to celestial beings.

SIGNS AND SYMBOLS

TALISMANS AND PENDANTS

The *skandola*, meaning official knife, is a talisman used to protect against evil. It is a magic signet ring that "bears incised representations of the lion, scorpion, bee (or wasp), and serpent. . . . It is worn [by the priest] during exorcisms and by those isolated for uncleanness, such as childbirth, or marriage."[2] This item is available only to priests, holy people, and laypersons who have been approved to assist in certain priestly functions. The *skandola* is used throughout the life cycle to ward away evil spirits. It is placed under a woman's bed during childbirth to protect the baby and take any evil from the baby.[3] It is used to seal newborns from evil, by impressing it on the baby's navel.[4] The bridegroom is invested with it by the priest during the wedding ceremony. The *skandola* is used during the funeral rites by attaching it first to the dead body until burial, and then to seal the tomb on all four sides after burial. It is even used for insomnia. The *skandola* also figures prominently in Mandaean legends of the battles in the underworld and between the various characters of mythology.

A symbol of particular interest is the *drabsa*, an emblem that looks similar to the Christian cross. The *drabsa* is a banner employed during the baptismal ritual. It is created by two cross-sticks, to which silk banners are attached, simulating celestial lights streaming to earth. Mandaeans make jewelry using the *drabsa* as a pendant and it is worn by both males and females.

2. Drower, *The Mandaeans of Iraq and Iran*, 37.
3. Wisam, interviewed by author 16 Oct 2006.
4. Drower, *The Mandaeans of Iraq and Iran*, 37–38.

Early missionaries encountered this symbol and assumed it was a cross, conveying the image of Christianity. However, this was a misunderstanding of the use of the *drabsa* during the baptismal ritual. Additional use of this symbol was identified by Ignatius of Jesus, a missionary in the seventeenth century, who noted that "little crosses [were] embroidered onto the priests' robes (going so far as to call them "the marks of priesthood"), even though they were hidden from sight for fear of the Moslems [sic]."[5] He also saw the Mandaean priests kissing the *drabsa* to demonstrate their devotion to it.

5. Lupieri, *The Mandaeans*, 89.

SIGNS AND SYMBOLS

Modern Mandaeans are preeminent jewelers with most young men learning the basics of this trade even if they pursue other vocations. The symbol looks like a Christian cross with a cloth draped over it, as is seen in some churches and especially during the Easter season. This wrapped cross is often confused as simply another version of the Christian cross, confusion not necessarily avoided nor corrected by modern Mandaeans any more than their ancestors. However, modern Mandaeans do not generally see it as a representation of their religion, nor of their baptism. Rather, it is considered a symbol of peace, and is worn to protect from evil and to bring good luck.[6]

CONCLUSION

Recognizing the elaborate systems that have been created to avoid evil and bring good luck and peace can be overwhelming, particularly in Western society where a worldview laced with superstition is not an inherent part of the culture. The legends, practices, and beliefs vary within the Mandaean community, based on what has been taught in the home. However, those from the priestly caste have greater exposure to these practices, and everything a priest does carries a price tag, so adherence and promotion of these practices is a prime concern of the priests. The lack of understanding of the legends and symbols by laypersons may be an advantage for spreading the gospel. On the other hand, dreams and visions are a common way in which the Holy Spirit has spoken to the hearts of people from the Middle East, so

---

6. Wisam, interviewed by author 16 Oct 2006. This was also stated by the Mandaean jeweler the author met in United Arab Emrites whose name is not released for security purposes.

recognizing that the Holy Spirit does still talk to individuals in this manner can be an advantage.

The *drabsa* is a very common accessory worn by children and adults, both male and female. While most Mandaeans simply see it as a good luck charm, a Christian's understanding of the symbolism of the *drabsa* and its role in the baptismal ritual of Mandaeans can present an opportunity for spiritual discussion with Mandaeans. The *drabsa* was misunderstood by early Roman Catholic missionaries in the sixteenth century because of its resemblance to the cross. Today's missionaries have the opportunity to be more perceptive to the true symbolism represented by the *drabsa*.

8

Conclusion: Opportunities

INTRODUCTION

THIS BOOK WAS INITIATED based on the premise that a better understanding of the Mandaean people and their beliefs would enhance the opportunity for the gospel to be shared with them in light of their unique circumstance as refugees who have emigrated from their native land in Iraq and Iran. As refugees, the Mandaeans are being dispersed throughout the world, unraveling their tight-knit community; the number of priests is dwindling, making it impossible to continue the Mandaean rituals in many locations; and the exodus of younger people from the sect exposes them to not only secular issues but also spiritual issues.

The fact that Mandaean beliefs are primarily taught within the family makes the information that is passed down inconsistent. Parents are often lacking in their own understanding and so are ill-equipped to instruct their children in this complex belief system. Furthermore, the information that is passed on is often questioned in light of the new realities faced by these people.

This concluding chapter will focus on specific apologetic approaches that might be used with this people group that is increasingly dispersed around the world. Most Mandaeans have limited knowledge of Christianity so it is important to find elements within their worldview that can serve as a bridge to the discussion of the gospel.

The issue of refugees is unlikely to abate in the foreseeable future. Officials initially thought the situation in Iraq would stabilize and previously displaced Iraqis would return to Iraq after 2006. However, the continued violence in Iraq has thwarted efforts to return and officials do not see this situation reversing for the foreseeable future.[1] Mandaeans leaving Iran usually depart under the pretext of visiting the European Union (EU), and then apply for asylum after their arrival. Once they are granted asylum, they may pursue immigration to other countries within the EU or throughout the world. Because they have felt the sting of living in a Muslim country, they are able to clearly document the marginalization they have felt in the land they have called home for centuries.

It is important to understand the belief system of this people group that has been inaccessible in the past. Understanding not only their physical needs as refugees but also their spiritual background is crucial, as the Mandaean belief system is likely to be unfamiliar to most Christians. For refugees, the two things they have usually been stripped of are hope and relationships. The Christian belief system not only brings hope for life after death; it mandates that Christians care for the poor, the oppressed, the broken-hearted, and those who are in physical need. By offering physical assistance, Christians have an opportunity to build relationships with Mandaeans that meet their basic needs at a time when it is most needed. Physical assistance, combined with true friendship and respect, provide a natural bridge for engaging in personal discussions. A significant investment of one's self is required when working with refugees, both temporally and emotionally. While meeting their immediate needs, a platform is being built to share spiritual beliefs.

Christians engaging Mandaeans may soon discover that many biblical names and events of the Bible are somewhat familiar to the Mandaeans. However, it will become evident that the names, places, and events are not usually portrayed from the biblical perspective. Since most Mandaeans cannot read their ancient holy books, they have obtained their worldview from oral communication, primarily passed down within families. Even if they have read their holy book, the *Ginza*, their understanding of the biblical characters will be distorted. Thus, much patience and understanding will be required of the Christian, who "must be careful not to speak with superiority about 'our faith' in such encounters. They should speak with humility."[2] Each encounter with an unbeliever must be bathed in prayer and conducted with love.

---

1. Associated Press, "Officials say about 100,000 flee Iraq monthly," 2.
2. "Christians, Muslims and the Communication of the Gospel," 450.

Conclusion: Opportunities

The literature speaks of many examples of natural disasters in recent times and the opportunities these have presented for the gospel. It becomes clear that without offering humanitarian aid there would have been no opportunity to earn the trust of those displaced in order to present the gospel. While nightly evangelistic meetings and distribution of scriptures in the language of the people may give the opportunity for the presentation of the gospel, it has been the humanitarian aid offered by Christians from different missionary organizations throughout the Middle East that has cultivated the hearts of people. "Christians in the Middle East are seeing a steady stream of . . . refugees become followers of Christ, often as a result of humanitarian aid offered by the Christians. . . . [They] are wide open to the Gospel in a way they haven't been before . . . and they are quite surprised by the help they are getting from the local Christians."[3] It is evident that works speak volumes before words are ever spoken.

STRATEGIES FOR DEVELOPING RELATIONSHIPS

Showing an interest in the culture, language, foods, habits, and practices of an individual goes a long way toward establishing trust and building friendships. The importance and significance of the English language cannot be overstated. Learning English is one of the most desirable things Westerners have to offer refugees in America and other countries, many of whom hope to immigrate to America or another English-speaking country someday. Even on short-term mission trips, one of the most requested tasks or services is to teach English. Teaching English provides the basis for developing trust, for building a relationship, for communicating, and for friendship. It also creates the stepping stones to introduce the gospel. Because learning English takes time, there is a progression in the relationship that naturally occurs and develops, ultimately providing a kinship that fosters sharing intimate values, including matters of faith. People of the Middle East, like all people, believe and trust those they know. It is crucial that a friendship relationship be developed as a first step toward sharing the gospel.

Research on Christian evangelism shows that in America "a person hears the gospel 3.4 times before they accept Christ."[4] For Muslims, it takes over one hundred contacts with the gospel "before the truth of it sinks in. And they have to hear it from different angles, in bits and pieces, until all of

---

3. Guthrie, "Gulf refugees respond to aid and gospel," 65–66.
4. Towns, *Winning the Winnable*, 13.

a sudden the pieces start falling together."⁵ Though no specific studies have been done on Mandaeans, it can be assumed it would take nearly as many contacts for Mandaeans as it does for the Muslims, given their country of origin, their Middle Eastern cultural disposition, and the inculcation of their own beliefs regarding spiritual things.

Chapter 1 of this book addressed the general distrust refugees have toward others: their native country, their new neighbors, others from their host country, and most especially, Westerners. An additional trust factor relates specifically to the Middle Eastern culture. Most socializing occurs in groups. However, one-on-one sharing is the only way to reach into the heart of a person from the Middle East. " . . . [T]hey will only share personal issues with someone they really trust, and this is rare. In the East, anything negative soon finds its way to the ears of friends and family. The result is shame and a loss of honor. . . . But there is a positive side to this. I have found that most Muslims living cross-culturally would rather share personal struggles with a Westerner than with another Muslim."⁶ Thus, being an outsider can be an advantage since deep spiritual issues will only be discussed in an atmosphere of trust, respect, and love.

APOLOGETIC APPROACHES FOR MANDAEANS

The most striking appeal to Mandaeans is in light of their most visible ritual, their repeated baptism, which is an effort to continually purify oneself in order to be prepared for the Lightworld. This continuous effort can be compared to the ritualistic traditions of the Old Testament. Indeed, many of their rituals, particularly the priestly ordination and some of the priests' responsibilities, are clearly reminiscent of the rituals and ordination process of the Old Testament. Yet, the Bible makes it clear that the rituals were not the saving mechanism; it was the heart that was turned toward God as reminded through the repeated rituals. Hebrews 10:3–7 describes the purpose of the sacrificial rituals as a reminder of sins, but what God really wanted was the hearts of the people, as indicated in Hebrews 8:10 and 10:8–16. Old Testament passages reinforce this concept, such as I Samuel 16:7, where God makes it clear he looks at the heart, and I Samuel 15:22,

---

5. Zoba, "Islam, USA," 50.
6. Hoskins, *A Muslim's Heart*, 23–24. This author deals specifically with Muslims, but his observations and comments apply to the culture of the Middle East. This viewpoint has been confirmed in conversations with missionaries and Mandaean converts.

Conclusion: Opportunities

where God indicates obedience is better than sacrifice. Galatians 3:23–25 further describes how the law, or rituals, was intended to lead us to Christ, not to achieve salvation. Finally, Romans 10:4 shows that Jesus was the end of the law, so there could be righteousness for all.

Another approach to a discussion of baptism and the once-for-all completion of the salvation process may be based on the symbol of the *drabsa*. An understanding of the origin and practical use of the *drabsa* as a part of the baptism ritual allows one to go beyond a simple discussion of the good luck charm to the reality of what the repeated baptisms are attempting to provide for the adherents. Since the repetitive baptisms are an attempt to purify oneself for admission to the Lightworld, the Redeemer's role in bringing people to heaven must be communicated. Acts 4:10 and 4:12 demonstrate there is no name other than Jesus that can bring salvation. John 14:6 quotes Jesus, who says he is "the way and the truth and the life. No one comes to the Father except though me." In Ephesians 2:8–9, Paul declares there is no salvation by works or human efforts.

The Mandaeans' effort to reunite with their celestial counterpart offers an opportunity to discuss the hierarchy of beings as created by God. The Bible chronicles the origin of Adam, who is their revered founder, as well as other honored prophets/celestial beings in their mythology, such as *Sitil* (Seth) and *Anus*. A discussion centered on the first eleven chapters of Genesis would bring light to the subject of Adam and his descendents, as well as his own need for salvation after sinning. A study of Romans five, and especially 5:12–21, clarifies the sinful nature of Adam that has been passed on to all generations. Further study in Hebrews 1:14, 2:5–12, and 9:27 demonstrates man's relationship to the angels, and the angels' relationship with God. Man's current relationship to the angels is below them on earth, but in heaven the angels are ministering spirits, serving the believers in heaven.

Recognizing that the Mandaean religion is a form of Gnosticism requires an understanding of gnostic dualism, the distinction of black and white as applied to all ethical and moral realities. Gnosticism cannot allow the good Supreme Being to exist without an equally supreme evil being. The Bible is clear that the evil of this world is subservient to God and that there is no greater power than that which God possesses. A study of the attributes of God reveals the holiness, righteousness, and justice of God.

The gnostic and Mandaean systems both rely on a redeemer. However, the ascension of Mandaeans to the heavenlies is not totally dependent on the redeemer. It is also dependent on the individual's human effort. On the other hand, scripture is clear there is only one who can deliver humans into the presence of God and that is Jesus Christ. It is by grace we are saved; it is not because of anything we have done or can do, but because of the penalty that Jesus has already paid for our sins, as stated in Ephesians 2:8–9 and Hebrews 9:27–28.

CONCLUDING THOUGHTS

While this book is focused on understanding the Mandaean belief system and presenting strategies and apologetic approaches to reach them with the gospel, it is important to recognize the Holy Spirit may already be working in the life of the Mandaean. Thus, it is the duty of Christians to provide compassionate humanitarian aid and to choose to love refugees unconditionally. The status of the Mandaeans as refugees casts them in the situation of needing material and financial assistance along with people upon whom they can depend. Factors that give Mandaeans a propensity toward the gospel are their interest in truth and their status as refugees, which may make them temporarily dependent upon others. Yet, the gospel is primarily demonstrated by actions before words. The following excerpt from the testimony of a young Mandaean woman exemplifies a common theme heard from several who are either missionaries to Mandaeans or Mandaeans who have converted to Christianity. That theme is the love and acceptance they received from Christians before they were ever presented with the gospel.

Dina was raised in a traditional Mandaean family in Iraq.[7] She confesses that at the age of ten, she was involved in things she wouldn't tell her parents about even years later. She was not aware of the religious beliefs, though her family did all the traditional rituals, including baptisms at least three times a year. There were no Mandaean books in her home and there was no specific form of prayer that she or her family knew of other than to simply speak if they wanted to talk to God. She had never heard the name of Jesus. Dina did not feel she received any spiritual upbringing within her family. (Interestingly, her uncle was pursuing priestly training at the same time, which illustrates the differences of training within the individual Mandaean homes.)

Dina had many opportunities to observe Muslims in her community and was especially aware of their frequent prayers. She also noted a lifestyle she considered wrong, as they tended to be selfish, greedy, dishonest, and to cheat. At her young age, she wondered, "What's the point of living?"

7. Dina, interviewed by author 10 Dec 2006. (Last name omitted for security purposes.)

Conclusion: Opportunities

While still in Iraq, Dina was reminded many times of her sins, which created a longing to reach God and know truth. Since she did not know how to pray to God in her Mandaean religion, she went to Islamic classes. Even as she tried to memorize the ninety-nine Islamic names of God, she longed to know God. Yet she was confused by the Muslims' hypocritical lifestyle and their lack of assurance of their own salvation.

When her family was forced to leave Iraq, they fled by cover of night and were dropped off by their driver in front of a Christian church and school in Amman, Jordan. They had connections in New Zealand and assumed their stay in Amman would last only a few weeks until they could emigrate. They didn't know anyone in Amman and needed to find housing quickly. They found a place, but it was owned by Muslims who would only rent to Muslims. In true Mandaean fashion, the family quickly adapted to the situation, with the father claiming they were Muslim.[8]

They rented the apartment, but after a few months they ran out of money. They could not work legally and the children could not attend school. Neighboring Muslim families provided cooked meals for them, often secretly leaving food at the door. Providing food for the family, sometimes in very bad weather, impressed Dina. (In retrospect, she notes that this occurred during Ramadan, a time when Muslims are supposed to be especially charitable to other Muslims. She also understood they were trying to get God's approval for their charity toward others.) Meanwhile, the Muslim landlords were pressuring Dina's father to attend the local mosque. Her father wanted to quit pretending so they began searching for another apartment.

The neighbors in their new apartment were Christians and the children were attending the nearby Christian school. Soon they invited Dina and her older sister to attend with them. Dina's mother had been a school teacher in Iraq, and when they discovered the school, she asked to volunteer as a teacher there so her children could go to school. The school, always in need of teachers, agreed, and Dina and her siblings enrolled in the Christian school. At the same time, the family moved from their apartment and began attending different functions of the church.

Dina said, "I was especially aware of the love, hope, and joy that the Christians had. While I felt the Muslims who had given food to my family were truly compassionate and not simply fulfilling an obligation, I sensed

---

8. Buckley, *The Mandaeans*, 27. It is not uncommon for Mandaeans to represent themselves as Muslims in order to get along. Buckley describes a situation of a family now in California who registered their children as Muslims while in Iraq for protection from discrimination and to provide access to higher education.

a different attitude among the Christians. When they sang, and when they prayed, it was as if their God really heard and answered them. When they provided physical aid, they credited it to Jesus in their lives. I had never heard this type of attribution before."

For Dina, it was ultimately God's Word that penetrated her seeking heart. She continued, "The pastor's message from the tenth chapter of the Gospel of John was the turning point for me. As he spoke of the "other sheep" that God knows and cares about, I saw myself as one of those "other sheep." I went home from church and prayed, asking Jesus into my life and to change my life." Dina's conversion led to most of her extended family becoming Christians. They eventually immigrated to Canada, where she graduated from a four-year Bible school.

It is ultimately the work of the Holy Spirit in a life that compels one to trust in Jesus Christ as the Savior of each individual soul. Missionaries who have seen Mandaeans come to Christ and Mandaean believers themselves have concurred that while the tragedy of their life circumstance makes them amenable to hearing the gospel, it is the love and compassion apparent in Christians which draws them to Christianity. As Dina succinctly stated, "I lived among Muslims all my life, but there was nothing in their lives that caused me to connect their actions with their beliefs or their God."

Mandy[9] came to know Jesus because of the kindness shown by a local American Christian, who volunteers to drive refugees to Omaha, Nebraska to take their citizenship test. Mandy came to the United States from Iran, via Vienna, Austria, where she spent four months as a refugee along with her family of four. Eventually, she ended up in Nebraska, where she felt there were more opportunities for refugees, such as English language training, legal and medical services, and friendly people.

She has assumed the name Mandy, meaning "Praise to God" because it was in Nebraska where she found Jesus Christ. Of their situation in Iran, Mandy says,

> At first it was very difficult to come to America because of the language. But I knew we had to leave our home in southern Iran and that the future would be better here for my family and me. We Mandaeans are a minority in Iran and it was very difficult to have a job in the Iran society. So, over the centuries, Mandaeans developed our own trade, which was making gold jewelry. Muslims can

---

9. Mandy, interviewed by author 04 Apr 2016. (Name changed for security purposes.)

Conclusion: Opportunities

wear gold, but they cannot work with it with their hands, so that became the major business of Mandaeans.

However, our children were forced to learn the Qur'an in school. We had to beg the teachers to give them a break because if they failed in the Islamic class, they could not go on to the next level.

In Iran, Mandy and her husband worked in a restaurant owned by Muslims, but they did not tell the owners they were Mandaeans. Eventually, their guilt overcame them, "so we told the owners; they thanked us for telling them. However, they said because we were working in the kitchen and serving food to Muslims, we could not continue to work there."

Mandy is an example of someone who encountered Jesus on more than one occasion before belief was established. She recalled,

When I was in Iran, I had heard about Jesus and had friends who were Christians. When they had church festivities I would attend with them. When I came to America, I had much more freedom, could attend church if I wanted. Here people are more open and this allowed me to seek, to ask questions. Nobody is forced to do anything here. I knew of other Mandaeans who became Christians, even in Iran. When they inquired about Christ, they decided to follow Christ.

I became a Christian in Nebraska. I knew a little about Christianity but when I travelled to Omaha to take my citizenship test, I met Amal. Amal drove refugees to Omaha to take their test, and that was the first time I met him. As he drove, Amal shared about Jesus to me. I understood that I can talk with Jesus about anything, any of my concerns. I decided to follow because I wanted a God who would listen to me and care about me. I didn't have that opportunity in my Mandaean religion. I started to go to church to hear and learn more. We are not taught our beliefs as Mandaeans, such as the story of John [the Baptist] and his special birth. Only the priests know the religion and its beliefs. They go through a long process of study and rites to become a priest. For me, I know that God exists and I come to him through Jesus Christ.

She continued to describe the relationship between the priests and the lay people in Mandaeism. "In my religion, there is a space between us and the leaders, who are the only ones who have a relationship with God. This relationship is not for the regular people. There were many rules that made for difficulties between the religious leaders and the people. The Bible and other Christian books opened our minds and we began to realize that

Christianity is better than what we knew before. Our minds have become open and we see this is better."

And confirming the importance of friendships with Americans, Mandy concluded, "Although I am alone in Nebraska, without family, I do not feel alone. My new Christian family has made me feel a part of them."

Bibliography

"Ancient religious group flees from Iraq; finds refuge in Mass." *Bennington (VT) Banner*, 7 Jul 2009.
Ankerberg, John, and John Weldon. *The Facts on Islam*. Eugene, OR: Harvest House, 1998.
Associated Press. "Ancient Iraqi Mandaean sect struggles to keep culture in Michigan," mlive, 1 Jul 2009, http://www.mlive.com/news/detroit/index.ssf/2009/07/ancient_iraqi_mandaean_sect_st.html.
———. "Officials say about 100,000 flee Iraq monthly," *The Roanoke Times*, 4 Nov 2006, sec. 2A, 2.
Bejjani, Amal. Discussion with author. 7 Mar 2005 and 27 Feb 2006.
Blume, Michael A. "Refugees and Mission: A Primer." *Mission Studies* 17 (2000) 162–72.
Bray, Gerald L. Review of *Gnosis and Faith in Early Christianity: An Introduction to Gnosticism*, by Riemer Roukema. *Churchman* 114 (2000) 92–93.
Buckley, J. J. "Glimpses of a Life: Yahia Bihram, Mandaean Priest." *History of Religions* 39 (1999) 32–49.
———. "Libertines or Not: Fruit, Bread, Semen and Other Body Fluids in Gnosticism." *Journal of Early Christian Studies* 2 (1994) 15–31.
———. "The Mandaean Appropriation of Jesus' Mother, Miriai." *Novum Testamentum* 35 (1993) 181–96.
———. *The Mandaeans: Ancient Texts and Modern People*. New York: Oxford University Press, 2002.
———. Review of *What is Gnosticism?*, by Karen L. King. *Journal of the American Academy of Religion* 72 (2006) 547–50.
———. "Why Once is Not Enough: Mandaean Baptism (*Masbuta*) as an Example of a Repeated Ritual." *History of Religions* 29 (1989) 23–34.
———. "With the Mandaeans in Iran." *Religious Studies News* 11. American Academy of Religion and the Society of Biblical Literature (1996) 8–11.
Caner, Emir, and Ergun Caner. *More than a Prophet*. Grand Rapids, MI: Kregel, 2003.
———. *Unveiling Islam*. Grand Rapids, MI: Kregel, 2002.
Caner, Ergun. "Doctrines of Islam." Lecture at Liberty Theological Seminary, Lynchburg, VA, 27 Oct 2005.
———. *When Worldviews Collide*. Nashville, TN: LifeWay, 2005.

Bibliography

"Christians, Muslims and the Communication of the Gospel." *International Review of Mission* 84 (1995) 447–52.

Cohn-Sherbok, Dan. "The Mandaeans and Heterdox Judaism." *Hebrew Union College Annual* 54 (1983) 147–51.

Coxe, A. Cleveland. *Ante-Nicene Fathers: The Writings of the Fathers down to A.D. 325.* Vol. 1: *The Apostolic Fathers, Justin Martyr, Irenaeus*, edited by Alexander Roberts and James Donaldson, 347–48. New York: Christian Literature, 1885.

de Blois, Francois. "The 'Sabians' in Pre-Islamic Arabia." *Acta Orientalia* 56 (1995) 39–61.

Drower, E. S. *The Mandaeans of Iraq and Iran.* Leiden, Netherlands: Brill, 1937.

Edwards, M. J. Review of *What is Gnosticism?*, by Karen L. King. *Journal of Theological Studies* 56 (2005) 198–202.

Eenigenburg, Donald M. Correspondence with author. 24 Jul 2006.

Flamm, Paul. "Refugee Ministry: Towards Healing and Reconciliation." *Mission Studies* 15 (1998) 99–125.

Franzmann, Majella. "Living Water Mediating Element in Mandaean Myth and Ritual." *Numen* 36 (1989) 156–72.

Geisler, Norman. "Beware of Philosophy: A Warning to Biblical Scholars." *Journal of the Evangelical Theological Society* 42 (2004) 3–19.

Gilhus, Ingvild. Review of *What is Gnosticism?*, by Karen L. King. *Numen* 51 (2006) 211–13.

Grant, Robert M., ed. *Gnosticism: A Source Book of Heretical Writings from the Early Christian Period.* New York: Harper & Brothers, 1961.

Gunduz, Sinasi. "The Problems of the Nature and Date of Mandaean Sources." *Journal for the Study of the New Testament* 53 (1994) 87–97.

Guthrie, Stan. "Gulf Refugees Respond to Aid and Gospel." *Christianity Today* 34 (1990) 65–66.

Halverson, Dean C. *The Compact Guide to World Religions.* Bloomington, MN: Bethany House, 1996.

Hamilton, Adam. *Christianity and World Religions.* Nashville: Abingdon, 2005.

Hanish, Shak. "Christians, Yazidis, and Mandaeans in Iraq: a survival issue." *Digest of Middle East Studies.* 18.1 (2009). http://ezproxy.liberty.edu/login?url=http://go.galegroup.com.ezproxy.liberty.edu/ps/i.do?p=AONE&sw=w&u=vic_liberty&v=2.1&it=r&id=GALE%7CA228662416&sid=summon&asid=aa752ec075fba90f56dc058f05fe0350.

Hedrick, Charles W., and Robert Hodgson, Jr., eds. *Nag Hammadi, Gnosticism, and Early Christianity.* Peabody, MA: Hendrickson, 1986.

Hoskins, Edward J. *A Muslim's Heart.* Colorado Springs, CO: Dawsonmedia, 2005.

Human Rights Watch. "Flight from Iraq: Attacks on Refugees and other Foreigners and their Treatment in Jordan." Human Rights Watch. 15 (2003).

Johnstone, Patrick. *Operation World.* Grand Rapids, MI: Zondervan, 1993.

King, Karen L. *What Is Gnosticism?* Cambridge, MA: Harvard University Press, 2003.

Kraeling, Carl Hermann. *Anthropos and Son of Man: a study in the religious syncretism of the Hellenistic Orient.* Vol 25. New York: Columbia University Press, 1927. Reprint, New York: AMS, 1966.

Lupieri, Edmondo. *The Mandaeans: The Last Gnostics.* Grand Rapids, MI: Eerdmans, 2002.

"Mandaeans." https://en.wikipedia.org/wiki/Mandaeism.

BIBLIOGRAPHY

"Mandaeans of Iraq since 2015." Mandaean Human Rights Group. March, 2017. www.mandaeanunion.com/images/MAU/MHRG/MHRG_Docs/The_Mandaeans_of_Iraq_Since_2015.pdf.

Mandryk, Jason. *Operation World*. Colorado Springs, CO: Biblica, 2010.

Marr, Phebe. *The Modern History of Iraq*. Boulder, CO: Westview, 2012.

McCarthy, Michael C. Review of *What is Gnosticism?*, by Karen L. King; *Theological Studies* 65 (2006) 639–41.

Mead, G. R. S. *The Gnostics: Fragments of a Faith Forgotten*. New Hyde Park, NY: University Books, 1960.

Miller, Jody. Email to author. 25 Jan 2006.

Mirecki, Paul A. Review of *What is Gnosticism?*, by Karen L. King. *Catholic Biblical Quarterly* 67 (2006) 349–51.

Moyise, Steve. Review of *Gnosis and Faith in Early Christianity: An Introduction to Gnosticism*, by Riemer Roukema. *Anvil* 17 (2000) 328–29.

Muhibbu-Din, M. A. "Ahl Al-Kitab and Religious Minorities in the Islamic State: Historical Context and Contemporary Challenges." *Journal of Muslim Minority Affairs* 20 (2000) 111–28.

Reinke, Sarah. "Mandaeans in Iraq." Inse Geismar and Yvonee Bangert, eds. The Society for Threatened Peoples, (2006) 8. http://www.gfbv.de/inhaltsDok.php?id=694 Accessed 13 Mar 2006.

Reuters. "Saddam praises Sabaeans, pledges to build temple," *Gulf News*, 12 Feb 2001. http://gulfnews.com/news/uae/general/saddam-praises-sabaeans-pledges-to-build-temple-1.415097.

Rorem, Paul. Review of *Hag Hammadi, Gnosticism, and Early Christianity*, edited by Charles W. Hedrick and Robert Hodgson, Jr. *Currents in Theology and Mission* 15 (1988) 286.

Roukema, Riemer. *Gnosis and Faith in Early Christianity: An Introduction to Gnosticism*. Translated by John Bowden. London: SCM, 1999.

Rudolph, Kurt. *Gnosis*. Translation ed. Robert McLachlan Wilson. New York: Harper & Row, 1983.

———. "Gnosticism: Shaping of Faith, Doctrine and Spirituality." In *Early Christianity: Origins and Evolution to AD 600: in honour of W.H.C. Frend*, edited by Ian Hazlett, 186–97. Nashville: Abingdon, 1991.

Schmithals, Walter. *Gnosticism in Corinth: An Investigation of the Letters to the Corinthians*. Translated by John E Steely. Nashville: Abingdon, 1971.

Segelberg, Eric. *Masbuta: Studies in the Ritual of the Mandaean Baptism*. Uppsala, Sweden: Almquist & Wiksells, 1958.

Sly, Liz. "Ancient Iraqi Sect is a Silent Casualty of War." *Chicago Tribune*, 16 Nov 2008. 1.9.

Smith, Carl B. *No Longer Jews: The Search for Gnostic Origins*. Peabody, MA: Hendrickson, 2004.

Smith, George D., ed. *The Teaching of the Catholic Church*. Vol. 1. New York: Macmillan, 1948.

———. *The Teaching of the Catholic Church*. Vol. 2. New York: Macmillan, 1949.

"Syria: Precarious existence of Iraqi Mandaean Community." *IRIN Middle East*, Damascus, 15 Sep 2010, http://www.irinnews.org/news/2010/09/15/precarious-existence-iraqi-mandaean-community.

Bibliography

Takona, Lilly A. "Strategies for Muslim Evangelization." *Africa Journal of Evangelical Theology* 15 (1996) 55–69.

Towns, Elmer. *Winning the Winnable: Friendship Evangelism*. Lynchburg, VA: Church Leadership Institute, 1986.

Williams, Michael A. *Rethinking "Gnosticism": An Argument for Dismantling a Dubious Category*. Princeton, NJ: Princeton University Press, 1996.

Wilson, R. McLachlan. *The Gnostic Problem: A Study of the Relations between Hellenistic Judaism and the Gnostic Heresy*. London: Mowbray, 1958.

Wisam. Interview with author. 16 Oct 2006.

Yamauchi, Edwin M. Review of *The Mandaeans: Ancient Texts and Modern People*, by J. J. Buckley. *Journal of the American Oriental Society*. 124 (2004) 136–37.

———. *Pre-Christian Gnosticism*. Grand Rapids, MI: Eerdmans, 1973.

Zoba, Wendy Murray. "Islam, USA: Are Christians Prepared for Muslims in the Mainstream?" *Christianity Today* 44 (3 Apr 2000) 40–50.

Index

Abatur (*also* Third Light), 28, 29, 31, 47, 50, 61, 62
Abel (*see* Hibil)
Abraham, 34, 35, 37, 54, 58, 63nii, 71, 72
Adam, 29, 30, 34, 35, 45, 48, 50, 51, 54, 55, 57, 61, 63nii, 71, 72, 85, 86, 87, 99
Afterlife (*see* Lightworld)
Ahl al-kitab (*see* People of the Book)
Anus, 29, 30, 31, 40, 60, 83, 85, 99

Baptism (*also* Masbuta, Immersion, Ritual Meal), 14, 32, 35, 39, 40, 41, 43, 44, 48, 50, 51, 55, 57, 59, 61, 64, 66, 67, 68, 69, 72, 74, 77, 79, 80, 81, 81n6, 82, 83, 85, 86, 87, 88, 89, 91, 92, 93, 94, 98, 99, 100

Calendar, (*see* Intercalary)
Catholic (*also* Catholicism, Portuguese missionaries), 2n2, 41, 42, 45niv, 87, 94
Celestial Beings (*see* Utra)
Celibate (*also* Celibacy), 33, 40, 41
Christianity (*also* Christian), xvi, 2, 2n2, 6, 9, 10, 14, 15, 16, 17, 18, 19, 22, 23, 24, 25, 26, 28, 31, 32, 35, 36, 39, 39n39, 40, 41, 47, 54, 55, 55n65, 56, 63nii, 66n7, 69, 71, 83, 85, 91, 92, 93, 95, 100, 102, 103, 104
Conversion, xi, xvi, 14, 29, 32, 34, 66, 102

Darkness, 14, 22, 24, 28, 29, 30, 31, 33, 52, 80, 89
Death (*also* Die, Dying), 21, 22, 23, 29, 30, 34, 41, 43, 45, 55, 57, 58, 61, 64, 67, 68, 69, 72, 74, 75, 81, 82, 85, 86, 87, 88, 90
Death Mass (*see* Masiqta)
Demiurge, 18, 19, 20, 60
Diaspora of Mandaeans, xvi, 4, 11, 14, 32, 64, 73, 80
Drabsa, 91, 92, 94, 99
Dualism, 19, 22, 30, 99

Euphrates River, 3, 10

First Life (*see* Great Life)
First Light (*also* King of Light), 27, 28, 30, 60
Funeral Ritual (*see* Masiqta)

Ganzibra, 44, 72, 73, 75, 85, 86
Ginza (*also* Left Ginza, Right Ginza), 10, 10n29, 26, 27, 30, 54, 58, 73, 81, 96

Index

Gnosis (*also* Knowledge, Secret Beliefs, Secret Knowledge, Secret Truth), xv, 12, 17, 20, 21, 22n37, 24, 25, 27, 28, 29, 33, 35, 48, 50, 51, 56, 57, 60, 72, 73, 74, 75, 89

Gnosticism (*also* Gnostic, Gnostics), xvi, 1, 4, 9, 10, 12, 15, 16, 17, 18, 19, 20, 21, 22, 23, 24, 25, 26, 27, 29, 31, 32, 33, 34, 35, 40, 66n5, 71, 73, 85, 99

Great Feast (*also* Dihwa Raba, New Year), 87

Great Life (*also* First Life, Lord of Greatness), 27, 28, 35, 60, 87

Heaven (*see* Lightworld)
Hell (*see* World of Darkness)
Hibil (*also* Hibil Ziwa), 29, 83, 87, 87n19
Hibil Ziwa (*see* Hibil)
Holidays, 32, 37, 43, 45, 51, 82, 87
Hussein, Saddam, xii, 5, 7, 47

Immersion (*see* Baptism)
Intercalary, 88, 88n20, 90
Iran (*also* Iranian(s)), xii, xiii, xv, 1, 3, 3n5, 4, 6, 10, 11, 12, 13, 14, 17, 47, 95, 96, 102, 103
Iraq (*also* Iraqi(s)), xii, xiii, xv, 1, 3, 3n5, 4, 5, 6, 7, 8, 10, 11, 12, 13, 14, 17, 41, 47, 64, 69, 76, 95, 96, 100, 101, 101n8
Islam (*also* Islamic), xvi, 2, 2n2, 5, 10, 15, 26, 32, 36, 40, 41, 42, 47, 48, 49, 51, 54, 55, 71, 85, 90, 101, 103

Jesus, 6, 11, 12, 20, 21, 22, 25, 28, 30, 31, 34, 39, 39n39, 40, 41, 42, 43, 44, 48, 55, 56, 57, 58, 59, 60, 61, 62, 63nii, 70, 71, 78, 99, 100, 102, 103
Jews, 20, 30, 36, 37, 38ni, 54, 55, 77ni
John the Baptist (*also* Followers of John the Baptist), xi, xiii, xv, 2, 2n2, 31, 35, 39, 39n39, 41, 45, 47n55, 57, 72, 85, 86, 90
Jordan River (*see* Yardna), 54, 59, 79

Judaism, xvi, 10, 15, 19, 23, 32, 35, 37, 41, 54, 55, 63nii, 71, 75, 78

Karun River, 3, 10
King of Light (*see* First Light)
Knowledge (*see* Gnosis)

Left Ginza (*see* Ginza)
Light, 22, 24, 28, 30, 31, 33, 39, 44, 57, 81, 82, 87, 87n19, 89
Lightworld (*also* Afterlife, Heaven), 20, 21, 22, 22n37, 23, 26, 27, 28, 29, 30, 31, 33, 34, 35, 39, 41, 43, 44, 45, 48, 52, 55, 58, 59, 60, 61, 67, 68, 69, 72, 75, 79, 81, 82, 83, 85, 86, 88, 90, 98, 99
Little New Year (*also* Short Feast, Dihwa Hnina), 87
Location of Mandaeans, 3, 4, 6, 11, 12, 36, 41, 54
Lord of Greatness (*see* Great Life)

Manda d-Hiia, 28, 29, 31, 38, 60, 62, 72, 85
Marriage (*also* Wedding), 5, 29, 32, 34, 44, 45, 50, 65, 66, 73, 85, 86, 91
Mary (Jesus' Mother), 31, 35, 36, 41, 42, 43, 44, 48
Masbuta (*see* Baptism)
Masiqta (*also* Death Mass, Funeral Ritual), 69, 74, 86, 87
Monotheistic, Monotheism, 10, 24, 36, 47, 50, 55, 60, 66n5
Moses, 58, 63nii, 71
Muhammad, 39, 54, 58, 85, 90

Nag Hammadi, 15, 16, 23
Names of Mandaeans, 2, 2n2, 2n3, 36
New Testament, 18, 63nii, 71, 78, 85
New Year (*see* Great Feast, Little New Year)
Noah, 57

Old Testament, 10n27, 19, 20, 21, 31, 37, 38, 38ni, 54, 55, 63nii, 71, 74, 77ni, 98

INDEX

Origin of Mandaeans (*also* Origin of Mandaean Beliefs), 10, 12, 13, 15, 16, 17, 18, 19, 20, 22, 22n37, 23, 26, 28, 30, 31, 35, 36, 39, 41, 54, 59, 72, 85, 99

Paruanaiia, 37, 38, 86, 87, 88, 88n20, 90
People of the Book (*also* Ahl al-kitab), 10, 35, 36, 42, 47, 49
Population of Mandaeans, 3, 4, 6, 7, 11
Portuguese (*see* Catholic)
Prayers, 10, 10n29, 16, 29, 32, 35, 43, 55, 58, 68, 74, 75, 77, 83, 85
Priest(s) (*see* tarmida, ganzibra), xii, 4, 6, 14, 27, 28, 29, 32, 33, 37, 38, 39, 41, 43, 44, 45, 48, 51, 64, 65, 66, 66n7, 69, 70, 72, 73, 74, 75, 76, 77, 77nix, 78, 79, 80, 82, 83, 85, 86, 87, 88, 91, 92, 93, 95, 98, 100, 103
Prophet(s), 21, 34, 36, 39, 40, 43, 47, 48, 57, 58, 63nii, 72, 85, 90, 99
Punishment (*also* Toll Booths), 28, 30, 43, 51, 68
Purgatory, 41, 68
Purification, 37, 39, 41, 43, 44, 45, 48, 74, 79, 85, 86, 88
Purity (*also* Impurity), 29, 30, 38, 45, 50, 51, 72, 74, 82

Qur'an, 2n2, 10, 36, 47, 50, 51, 52, 52nv, 54, 55, 58, 59, 62, 103

Right Ginza (*see* Ginza)
Ritual Meal (*see* Baptism)

Sabaeans (*see* Names)
Sabba (*see* Names)
Sabi (*see* Names)
Sabians (*see* Names)
Salvation, 21, 25, 33, 36, 39, 41, 45, 50, 55, 65, 66, 68, 70, 81, 89, 99, 101
Secret Beliefs (*see* Gnosis)
Secret Name, 67, 81
Secret Truth (*see* Gnosis)
Secretive (community), 2, 5, 21, 23, 29, 51
Seth (*see* Sitil)
Shem, 57, 63nii, 71, 72
Short Feast (*see* Little New Year)
Sitil (*also* Seth), 29, 30, 57, 72, 83, 99
Skandola, 91
Soul, 21, 22, 22n37, 24, 26, 30, 33, 34, 41, 43, 45, 48, 52, 55, 61, 68, 85, 86, 88, 89, 90
St John Christians (*see* John the Baptist)
Subba (*see* Names)
Sunday, 40, 43, 48, 51, 55, 59, 67, 82, 85
Syncretism (*also* Syncretic, Parasitism), xvi, 23, 27, 32, 34, 54, 71

Tarmida(s), 43, 44, 48, 69, 72, 73, 74, 75
Third Light (*see* Abatur)
Tigris River, 3, 10
Torah, 37, 38, 58
Trinity (Mandaean), 29, 55, 83

Underworld (*see* World of Darkness)
Utra, Utria, 27, 28, 30, 83, 90

Wedding (*see* Marriage)
World of Darkness (*also* Underworld, Hell), 28, 48, 52, 55, 68, 87, 89, 91

Yardna, 59, 60, 79

www.ingramcontent.com/pod-product-compliance
Lightning Source LLC
Chambersburg PA
CBHW050837160426
43192CB00011B/2066